THE
NORTH LIGHT
ILLUSTRATED
BOOK OF
WATERCOLOR
TECHNIQUES

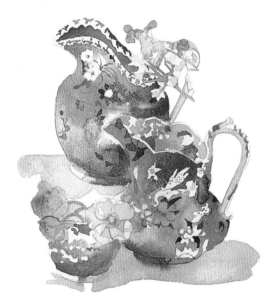

THE
NORTH LIGHT
ILLUSTRATED
BOOK OF
WATERCOLOR
TECHNIQUES

Mark Topham

NORTH
LIGHT
BOOKS

Cincinnati, Ohio

To my wife Lola and my daughter Bianca

A QUARTO BOOK

First published in North America
in 1997 by North Light Books,
an imprint of F&W Publications, Inc.,
1507 Dana Avenue, Cincinnati, OH 45207
1-800/289-0963

ISBN 0-89134-780-1

This book was designed and produced by
Quarto Publishing plc
The Old Brewery
6 Blundell Street
London N7 9BH

Senior Editor *Kate Kirby*
Senior Art Editor *Penny Cobb*
Designer *Giles Davies*
Photographers *Chas Wilder, Laura Wickenden*
Picture Researcher *Miriam Hyman*
Picture Manager *Giulia Hetherington*
Editorial Director *Mark Dartford*
Art Director *Moira Clinch*

Typeset by Central Southern Typesetters, Eastbourne
Manufactured by Regent Publishing Services Ltd, Hong Kong
Printed by Leefung-Asco Printers Ltd, China

Previous spread:
Alan Oliver, Tuscan Village.

FOREWORD

With any medium, the first stage is to learn to understand its physical nature. If you are coming to watercolor from another medium, particularly an opaque one such as oils, you will need to discover how watercolor differs. Once you have gained a full knowledge of what the medium can and cannot do, you will be able to use it fluently and with confidence, turning its unique properties to the all-important task of expressing your own ideas.

This book aims to help you toward a full understanding of this delightful and versatile medium. The book begins with a short introductory chapter explaining what you will need in order to make a start, including some useful tips on choice of paper and colors. So that you can follow a logical learning curve, the remainder is divided into two main sections, the first dealing with the basic techniques such as laying washes, blending colors, and reserving highlights, and the second introducing you to a selection of the watercolor painter's "tricks of the trade."

This painting uses gum arabic – one of many special techniques explained in the section starting on page 80.

One of the great charms of the medium is that it refuses to be completely tamed, often producing unexpected results. Some of the special techniques covered in the second section show you how you can take advantage of these accidental effects, for example, turning backruns and haphazard blotches into an exciting feature in your painting. Others demonstrate methods of suggesting texture and adding surface interest, both of which can be problematical with a fluid and transparent medium like watercolor. You will learn several different ways of creating highlights, including masking, using opaque white paint, and lifting out (removing paint from the paper). Watercolor can be successfully combined with other media, and this section also explores the possibilities of mixed-media work as well as the time-honored line and wash method.

Each technique is illustrated with step-by-step sequences showing its application for a variety of subjects: landscape, portraits and still lifes.

Each technique is illustrated with step-by-step sequences showing its application for a variety of subjects. These demonstrations are backed up by specially chosen and carefully annotated finished paintings which enable you to see how individual artists have adapted the methods to suit their subject matter and personal approach. Always remember that techniques are a means to an end – the result justifies the method and the method determines the result.

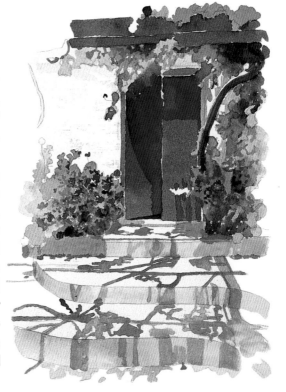

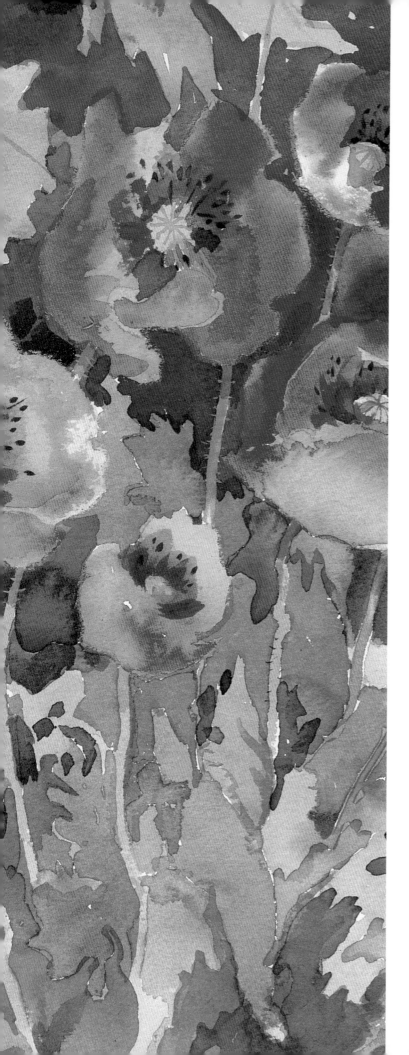

CONTENTS

BEFORE YOU START

The three essentials for watercolor painting are paints, brushes, and paper. There is a wide range of tools and materials available. But the beginner doesn't need a huge kit to get started. This section describes what you will need before you put paint to paper.

BASIC TECHNIQUES

The watercolor artist has a huge range of techniques to call on ranging from perfectly laid washes to scratched back highlights. In this section we look at the basic techniques available to the artist.

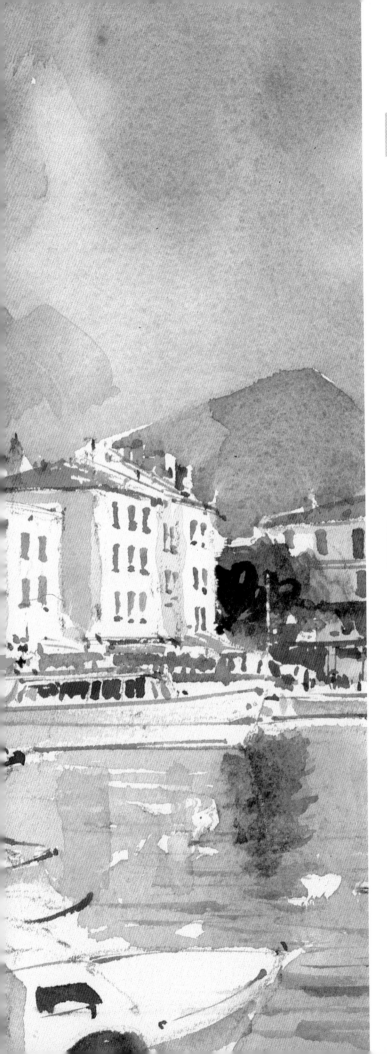

SPECIAL TECHNIQUES

This section looks at special techniques – the watercolor painter's "tricks of the trade." One of the great charms of the medium is it refuses to be completely tamed. Some of the techniques in this section show you how to take advantage of this. Each technique is demonstrated with step-by-step sequences showing its application for a variety of subjects.

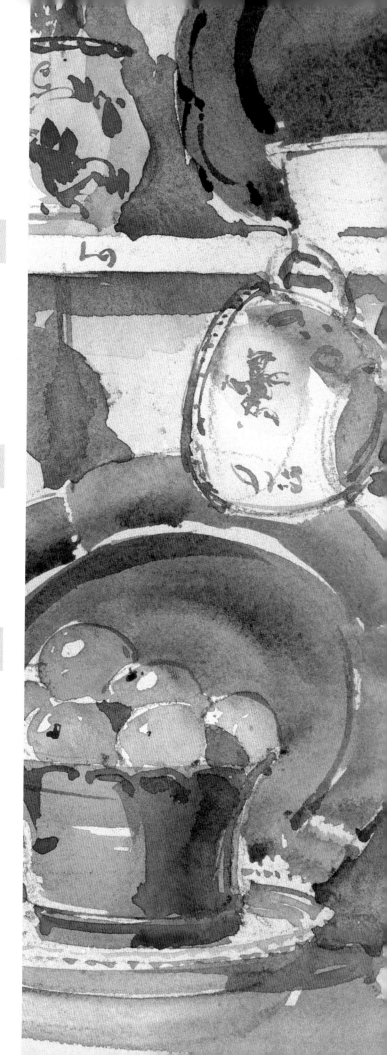

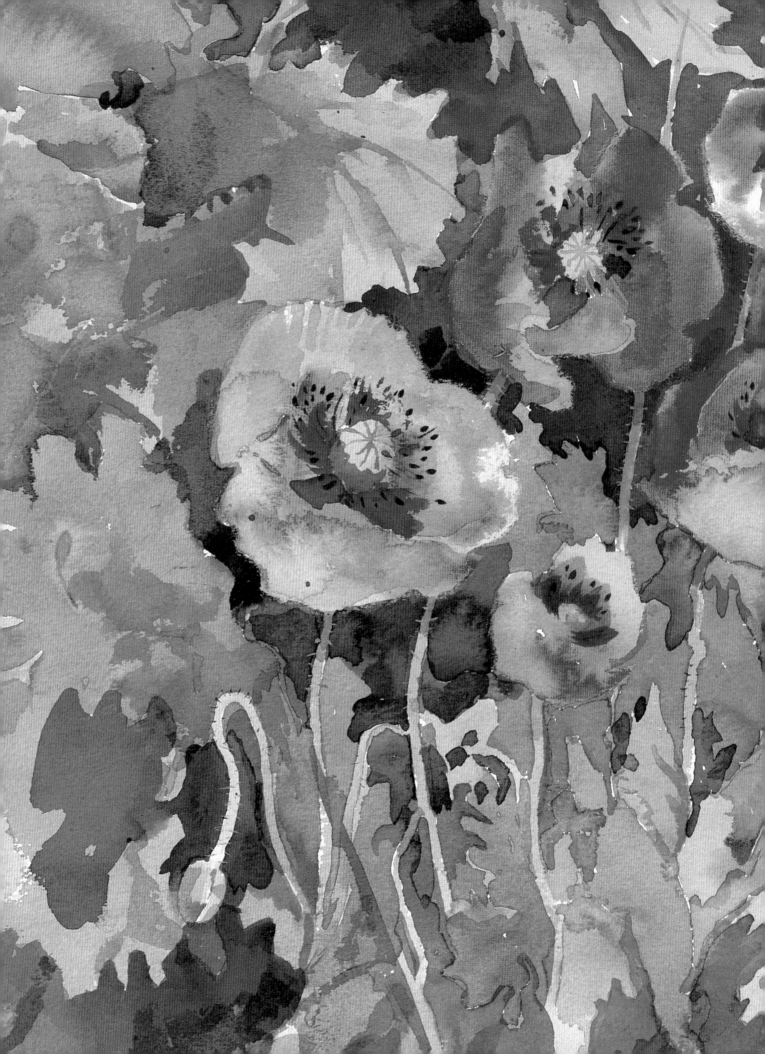

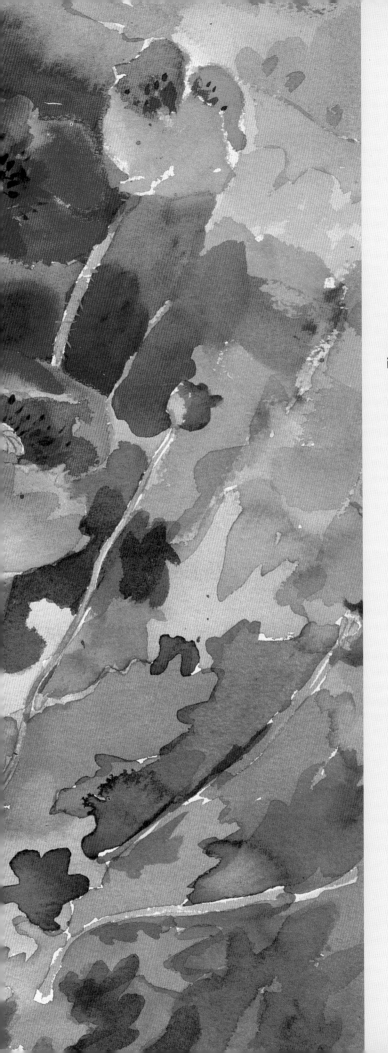

BEFORE YOU START

The three basic essentials for watercolor painting are paints, brushes, and paper. There is a wide range of paints available, and a huge choice of colors; brushes can be flat or round and come in different sizes; and paper is sold in different thicknesses and textures. The beginner doesn't need a huge kit to get started. In this section we describe what you will need and some of the principles you will need to understand before you put paint to paper.

Garden Poppies
Maurice Read

Basic equipment

The range of equipment on display in art shops is immense, and can be bewildering to the beginner. But you need surprisingly little to produce a watercolor painting, indeed watercolor is one of the simplest mediums in terms of materials, all of which are lightweight and portable, and can be used outdoors as easily as in. These tools will be sufficient for the techniques shown in Basic Techniques, with the exception of highlights (see pp.62–5).

Watercolor paints are made in different qualities and different forms for the varied uses of the medium. The two qualities can be divided into "student's" and "artist's," the latter being in the main made from superior pigments and thus more expensive. You could begin by experimenting with student's paints and progress to artist's quality as your confidence grows and you feel able to tackle more advanced work, but it is wiser to invest in quality from the outset.

TYPES OF WATERCOLOR

Watercolor paints are produced in three main forms, pans, tubes and bottles, the first two being the most popular. Each has its own advantages. It takes longer to release paint from a pan than to squeeze it from a tube, so tubes allow you to mix up larger washes, as well as giving greater scope for varying the consistency. But the pans come in boxes, with the lid serving as a palette, which is more convenient for outdoor work – if you use tubes you must take a separate palette. Pans in boxes are often used for smaller paintings and outdoor sketches. The paint, if artist's quality, always remains slightly moist, quickly releasing color onto a wet brush.

To begin with you will need at least one small pointed brush, a size 3 or 4, one medium and one large wash brush. Again there is a large range, made from a variety of natural and artificial fibers. Sable brushes are the most expensive and the best, springy and hard wearing, but synthetic brushes are a reasonable alternative for initial attempts, and softer brushes, such as ox or squirrel hair, can be useful on occasions.

Even if you are using a watercolor box with its own palette, you may need another one as well; the palettes with only small pans can be restrictive. My preferred palette has many small pans for squeezing out paint and large compartments for mixing with plenty of freedom. Apart from the many plastic or porcelain palettes available, many plastic disposable food containers and white plates and saucers make excellent alternatives.

It's a good idea to use two water containers, a large one for rinsing brushes and a smaller one which you can refill for a clean supply of water. To carry water for outdoor work, a lightweight plastic container with a lid is ideal.

Paints

1 Tubes *contain concentrated paint of a thick consistency, ready for dilution with water. They are priced according to a grading system, with some colors being more expensive than others.*
2 *Good-quality moist **pans** will immediately release color onto a wet brush. During color mixing they inevitably become contaminated with other colors, and have to be cleaned.*

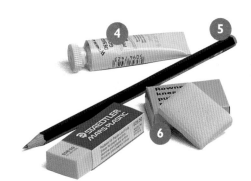

3 Paint box *Each pan can be replaced when finished. A little space between pans will reduce contamination of adjacent colors. The palette is small and will need regular cleaning with tissue paper during use to ensure purity of colors.*

Even if you are using a watercolor box with its own palette, you may need another one as well.
4 White gouache *This is a very concentrated opaque white. Mixing it with watercolors makes them opaque, a medium known as body color. White gouache is often used for highlights and finishing touches.*

Pencils

5 Pencils *range from 6H (very hard) to 9B (very soft). As the number increases the graphite becomes softer, creating progressively darker lines. For the initial underdrawing for a watercolor, artists normally use a range from HB to 4B.*

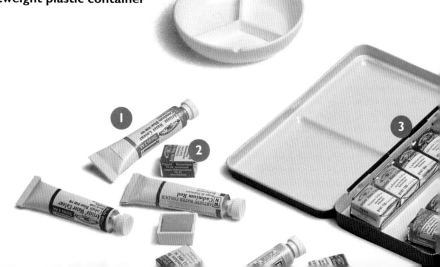

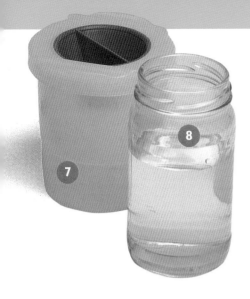

Palettes

9 *Instead of one large, cumbersome palette, you can use several* **small saucers**. *These are convenient to maneuver, as you can bring the ones in use closer. Some have separate compartments for small mixes, while others are open for larger washes. They are only suitable indoors on a work surface.*

10 Porcelain palettes *with smooth surfaces on which the paint flows and mixes with ease, are pleasant to work on, but their weight and fragility restricts them to indoor work.*

Brushes

11 Round *These are usually synthetic or sable. The best quality is the sable, which will always return to its original shape with a fine point. It is the easiest brush to begin with. The best sizes to start with are a no. 3 and no. 10.*

12 Rigger *This is a long, thin variety of the round brush, made of either synthetic fibers or sable. Designed for extended fine lines, it is traditionally used by marine artists. The long hairs allow extra control, with less susceptibility to hand shake. It's also ideal for brush drawing.*

13 Oriental brushes *Made from deer's hair, these are an economical addition to a kit. They are ideal for a calligraphic style of painting, but with practice will produce a wide variety of brushmarks. The hairs become springy when wet, and will hold any particular shape you may require.*

14 Long flat *Usually produced in ox hair or synthetic, which have different characteristics. The synthetic has finer hairs and is more springy, but the ox hair will last longer and produces a wide variety of brushstrokes on a textured surface.*

15 Mop brush *A squirrel soft-hair brush, mainly used for large washes or used for general painting on a large scale, producing a loose freehand effect.*

16 Small hog's hair *As well as applying paint, this is mainly used for scrubbing the painted surface with water, to loosen the pigment for lifting off. As it wears down, the hairs can be clipped to keep them firm.*

17 Hake *A reasonably priced wash brush with ox hair. With a little practice this can become an invaluable addition to the kit. It is used for laying broad washes.*

18 Decorator's brush *These come in many sizes and qualities. Some better ones, notably one made of cactus fibers, can be used as wash brushes, with stiffer hairs producing rich textured effects.*

Erasers

6 *There is a variety of* **erasers** *available, which work in different ways. The "putty" type used by many professional draftsmen has to be kneaded slightly then lifts of the graphite, pastel or charcoal by absorbing it. Traditional soft erasers leave a residue, which must be brushed off the paper. The hard eraser works like fine sand paper, rubbing off with friction.*

Water containers

7 Plastic containers *with watertight lids are good for outdoor work. They are lightweight for carrying, and brushes can be rested in the special troughs on the top.*

8 Household glass jars, *thoroughly cleaned, make ideal water containers. The clear glass allows you to check the purity of the water, and change it when necessary.*

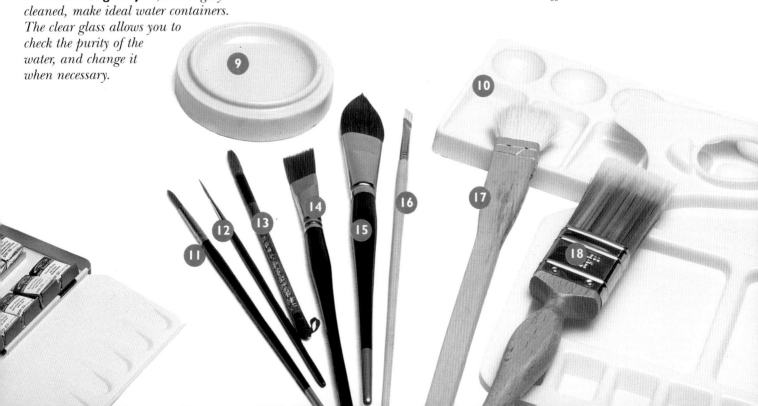

Special equipment

Later in the book you will explore some special techniques and more unusual methods, and the equipment given here reflects the need to experiment, and in some cases to "borrow" equipment and techniques from other fields.

Some of the items shown, however, such as a hairdryer, tissue, gumstrip, and masking fluid, are extensions to your basic kit. Others would be used rarely as the need arises, for example, salt.

1 Hairdryer *A small low-powered one will suffice, with a long flex. Used for drying intermediate washes and to speed up the process of stretching paper. Care must be taken when using electricity in such proximity to activity with water.*

2 Masking tape *For masking the outside edge of the picture to leave a clean edge. Also as a straight-edge mask during painting (see p.92). It has low adhesion and will not tear the paper when peeled off.*

3 Gumstrip *Used for stretching paper. Use 2-in-wide strip to withstand the stresses of paper stretching.*

4 Small natural sponges *Can be used for lifting off wet paint, or for applying it, to produce fine irregular patterns.*

5 Cotton buds *Perfectly suited for lifting off fine areas of wet paint for highlights, as they absorb quicker than a brush.*

6 Masking fluid *Liquid rubber solution, which is painted on to protect the selected areas from paint. It has a short shelf life, becoming*

discolored and separating out, so should be used within a few months.

7 Synthetic sponges *Ideal for wetting down the paper. Small pieces can be torn off for texturing effects.*

8 Tissue *Absorbent tissue has several uses, including keeping the palette clean during painting, cleaning brushes, lifting off, and removing stray splashes. Highlights and cloud effects can be produced by lifting out paint with crumpled tissue (see p.40).*

9 Board *Should be lightweight and resistant to warping. Thin-cross plywood is best suited to the purpose.*

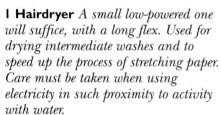

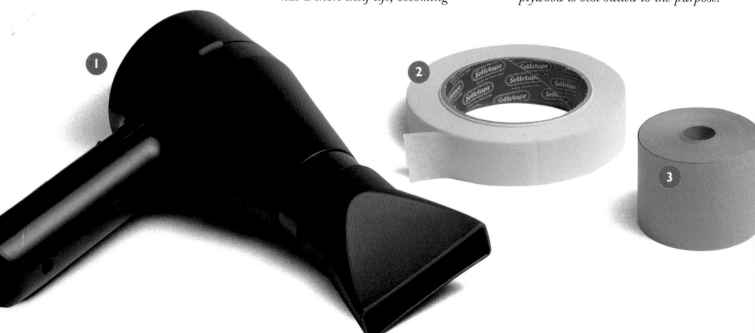

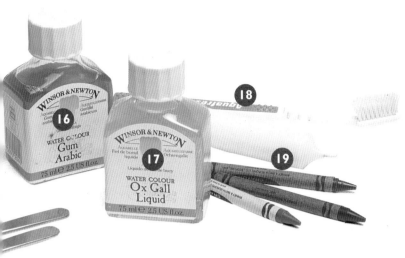

16 Gum arabic *A viscous medium that can be added to a paint mixture to thicken it slightly and give it a slight sheen. It does not sacrifice the transparency of color.*

17 Ox gall liquid *A wetting agent that increases the volatility of watercolor and causes it to flow more freely.*

18 Toothbrush *An excellent tool for spatter effects. Its shape allows you to point it at the chosen area and pull your finger over the bristles to produce a fine spray.*

19 Wax crayons *and* **candle** *Either of these can be used for resist methods, in which paint is laid over wax. The wax repels the water, so color will settle only on the non-waxed areas.*

Other equipment

10 Painting knife *For applying thick paint and for knifing out. Different shapes and sizes are available. The one shown here has a rounded point.*

11 Ruler *Used in conjunction with a pencil or brush for straight lines, and with a scalpel and masking tape for accurate straight-edged masking.*

12 Rock salt *Special textures can be achieved with salt. Coarse-grained salt is best, although it needs time to work. It can be crushed to make finer crystals.*

13 Indian ink *A very concentrated black, mainly used in line and wash or drawing. It usually comes in small jars, but can also be bought in the traditional stick form.*

14 Nib pen *The least expensive is a mapping pen, but drawing pens with interchangeable steel nibs are advised for the best results.*

15 Scalpel *Can be fitted with a curved or straight blade. The pointed blade is best for cutting paper and scratching out fine lines. The curved blade will scratch out larger areas.*

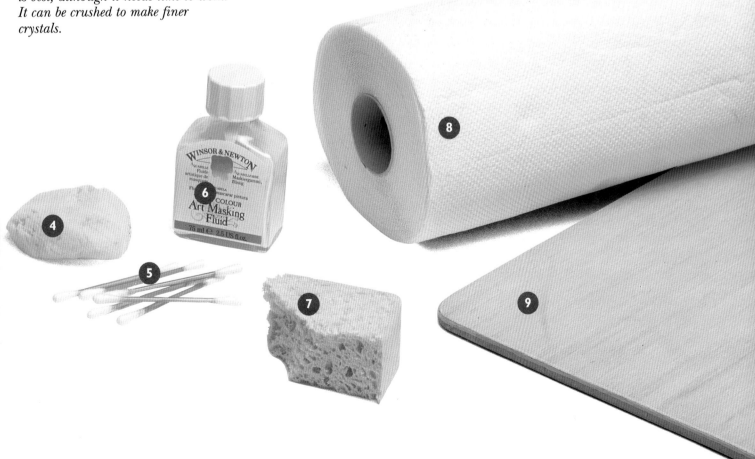

Paper

Watercolor paper can either be bought in pads of various sizes or in large sheets which are then cut down to the size you require. The former are more expensive, but convenient for outdoor sketching. The paper is made in three different surfaces: smooth, medium, and rough. The smooth paper is known as hot pressed (HP), because it is produced with heat and under pressure. This is also available as watercolor board, which is often used by illustrators, as it removes the necessity for stretching. The medium paper, the most commonly used, is called "not," short for "not hot pressed." Rough paper is known only by their name. It has a coarse texture liked by some artists, but is not the easiest for beginners. Specialist suppliers also stock handmade papers, which do not conform to the above categories, and all have their own special characteristics. There are also tinted papers, which are made with a faint color bias.

PAPER THICKNESS

Another variation in papers is their thickness, which is expressed in pounds, referring to a ream of 500 sheets. The thinner paper (140lbs or below) is cheaper, but needs to be stretched before use or may buckle and warp when you wet it, and will dry in the same condition. Cartridge paper can also be stretched. This is an inexpensive alternative to watercolor paper if you like a smooth surface. Paper above 200lbs does not require stretching.

Pads of watercolor paper are often made in the form of blocks. Each sheet has to be torn away on all sides to remove it, which has a similar effect to stretching. It is not quite as effective, but the pads are easier for outdoor work.

Hot-pressed paper is either completely smooth or has a very fine-grained texture. It is the most suitable paper for pen and line work. It is less absorbent than other papers, so wet paint may pool, and washes dry with hard edges.

▶ **Sketchbooks**
You should have two different sizes: one small one with cartridge paper for quick pencil sketches and light washes, and an A4 pad of watercolor paper for more complete paintings.

Stretching paper

If you have tried watercolor painting on fairly thin paper, you will have noticed its tendency to buckle when you apply wet washes, and then to dry unevenly, in a series of waves. This is due to the rapid expansion of the paper when wet, a tendency which you can turn to your advantage. If you tape it down when wet and fully expanded, it will shrink as it dries, pulling itself taut as a drum, producing a lovely springy surface not unlike a canvas.

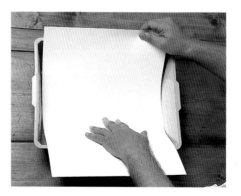

1 The paper must be fully submerged in water for a few moments, either in the bath or sink or slowly passed through a large bowl, as shown here. This ensures that every inch of both sides is thoroughly wetted.

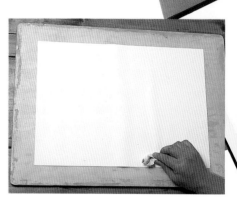

2 Take the paper out of the water, still dripping wet, and lay it on the board in position to be stretched. Leave it for a few minutes for the water to be completely absorbed, and when the buckling process has reached maximum, mop off surplus water with tissue. Then pull the paper at one end, holding the other end down.

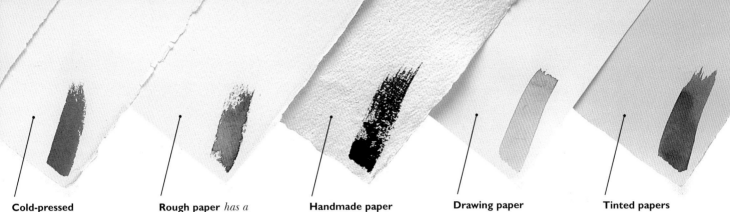

Cold-pressed paper, often referred to as "Not" paper standing for "not hot pressed," is the most commonly used. It has enough texture to hold the paint well, but will still allow for fine brushwork.

Rough paper *has a more pronounced grain, resulting in looser and more textural brushwork. This is not recommended for the beginner, but can be very exciting to use when you become more experienced.*

Handmade paper *is made in a variety of weights and surfaces. It can be even more unpredictable than a Rough paper, and is only recommended for the more experienced. It is also more expensive than machine-made papers.*

Drawing paper (cartridge paper) *This is the least expensive paper, mainly used for drawing. It will accept watercolor, but being lightweight, will need stretching. Drawing paper in sketchbook form is adequate for light washes.*

Tinted papers *These are a version of normal watercolor paper, but made in an overall even, pale color. The one shown here is a tinted hot-pressed paper. If you cannot obtain these papers, you can tint your own with a flat wash of diluted acrylic paint.*

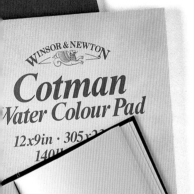

WINSOR & NEWTON

Cotman
Water Colour Pad

12x9in · 305x2...
140...

▶ **Watermarks**
Even though you can paint on both sides of most good-quality papers, there may be a slight difference in texture. If you hold the paper up to the light and read the watermark, you can check which is the correct side.

3 Dry the edges of the paper where the gumstrip will go with some fresh tissue, then cut the strip into lengths, wet the sticky side with a damp sponge, and stick down.

4 When all four sides are taped down, use more tissue to wipe over the top of the gumstrips. Press it down to squeeze out any excess water and ensure a good adhesion between the two surfaces. Also mop up any nearby pools of water which could run into the gumstrip, dissolving the glue and weakening the adhesion.

5 Leave the paper to dry for a few hours, or if you are in a hurry, speed up the process with a hairdryer. It is advisable to check on it during drying; if one side has not stuck properly, you can reinforce it with a fresh piece of gumstrip.

Before you paint

There are two main approaches to developing a painting. You can "work it up" from photographs and sketches done on the spot, or you can paint direct from life. There are important benefits to the direct approach.

You will acquire the ability to translate a three-dimensional scene into the two dimensions of your piece of paper. You will develop skills in composition, because rarely will you find the perfect composition handed to you without the necessity for modification, alteration or simplification. And you may see more possibilities in your subject than a photograph would reveal. When you are sketching you are inevitably studying your subject carefully, and viewing it from different angles. Even if your efforts do not result in the ideal painting, it will have been a valuable learning exercise.

Making a start

The bare minimum you need to make a start, and jot down visual ideas, is a sketchbook and pencil, together with a small watercolor box to enable you to add color washes to your drawing. You can then progress to a watercolor pad, producing more complete paintings from life.

A range of photographs can be collected as a form of reference library, which you can draw on for ideas. Photographs are also ideal for capturing short-lived effects; this still-life photograph records the moment the sun streamed through the window, an excellent back-up reference for a painting.

The camera is perfect for note-taking on scenery, when you don't have time to stop.

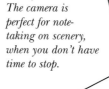

Fast action, which might otherwise be missed, can be easily frozen with the camera.

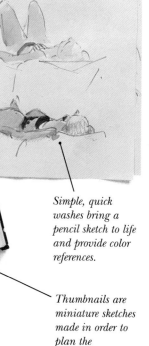

A sketch can become a finished work in its own right, like a camera catching a fleeting light effect or the expression on a face.

Simple, quick washes bring a pencil sketch to life and provide color references.

Thumbnails are miniature sketches made in order to plan the composition.

Viewfinder

Cut out a rectangular window from cardboard of a neutral color, such as black or gray. With a pencil, mark quarter segments on two sides and half segments on the others. These marks will aid in calculating the proportions of different objects.

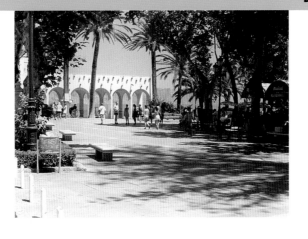

Measuring

It's common for simple but fundamental mistakes to go unnoticed until it is too late to make substantial changes, so try to get the drawing right before you begin to paint. Your pencil can play a dual role. As well as drawing with it, you can use it to check angles and work out the relative sizes of objects.

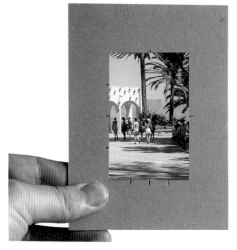

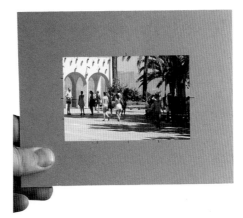

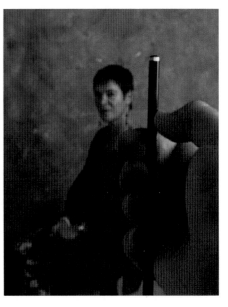

Hold the pencil at arm's length and slide your thumb up and down it to calculate the relative sizes of objects.

▲ *By holding up the viewfinder, you can eliminate surrounding detail, simplifying the scene and helping you to make decisions on what to include in your picture, and what format to choose. You can also more easily calculate the various proportions, by checking where the verticals, horizontals, and diagonals meet the inner edge of the veiwfinder.*

▲ *This shows the possibilities of a landscape format. You can spend time moving the viewfinder around at arm's length, trying out first a landscape format and then a portrait shape, until the composition begins to take shape. As you start painting refer back to the viewfinder to double check the proportions.*

▼ *When working outdoors the simple window-type viewfinder is the simplest to use, but if you want to vary the proportions from a standard rectangle, two cut-out "L" shapes can be used. This allows you to plan a square composition, or an elongated landscape shape, as shown here.*

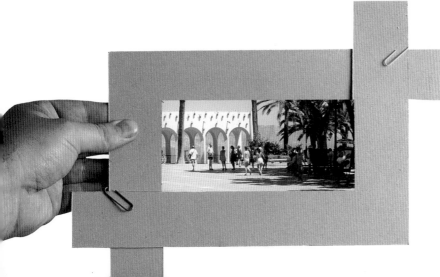

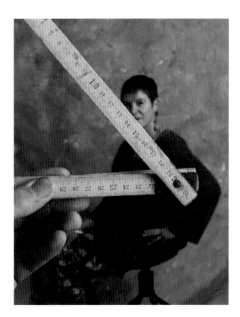

Hold up the wooden ruler and swivel it till it matches the diagonal, then transfer the line to the drawing.

Studio painting

Once you have gained experience of working "in the field" you will be able to use your outdoor sketches as a basis for indoor compositions, which can be more carefully controlled, and returned to over a period of time. If you are sketching in a monochrome medium such as pencil, make color notes to help you when you come to carry out the finished painting. The camera, which is an excellent tool for gathering information and recording effects of light, can be used as a backup for sketches, but you should avoid becoming too reliant on photographs, as this can stifle your creativity.

Begin by spreading out your store of visual references made on the spot, and then make a few further sketchbook studies to plan the composition and structure before embarking on the painting. These can be quite small – the smallest sketches are called thumbnails but can quickly establish the basics. You can try out color combinations at this same planning stage. Working closely in a sketchbook gives you more freedom to make mistakes. You can construct the painting in advance through trial and error, so that once you start on it you will know exactly what you are doing.

Page 18 shows some thumbnail sketches of this subject, which were done on location, together with this drawing. The thumbnails established the format and composition, while this drawing provides all the detail needed for the finished painting.

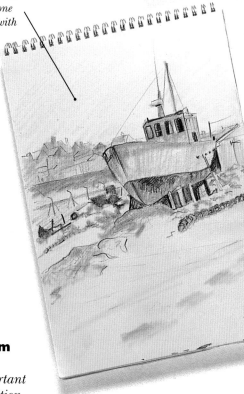

▶ **Working from sketches**
All the most important aspects of composition, including the relative sizes and positions of the elements and the distribution of tones, are established at the beginning, in this case during the drawing stage. With all this out of the way you have more freedom later to concentrate on color.

Enlarging with a grid

Preliminary sketches are often drawn smaller than the finished painting, as they are usually done in sketchbooks; to make them full size would be unnecessary. If you are working from photos, they will also need to be enlarged. This can be done solely by eye, but this is difficult to enlarge accurately, as the eye plays tricks. The grid method is an accurate way to transfer, enlarge, reduce or even deliberately distort an image. It is time-consuming, but you can be sure of accurate proportions. You will need to draw two grids, one to go over the reference and a second, proportionately larger, to act as a guide for the new drawing.

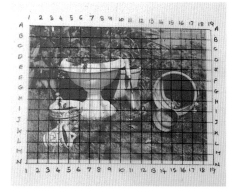

1 Lay a sheet of tracing paper over the sketch or photo and tape the two together at the back with masking tape. Using a ruler and set square, draw a grid of equal squares over the whole of the tracing paper. Number each vertical line and letter each horizontal line, so that you can fix any point of reference.

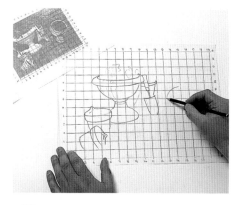

2 This drawing is being enlarged twice up from the original. Take another larger sheet of tracing paper and redraw the grid, exactly twice the size, then label the squares in the same way with numbers and letters. Transfer the drawing from the small to the large grid, using clear, simple lines.

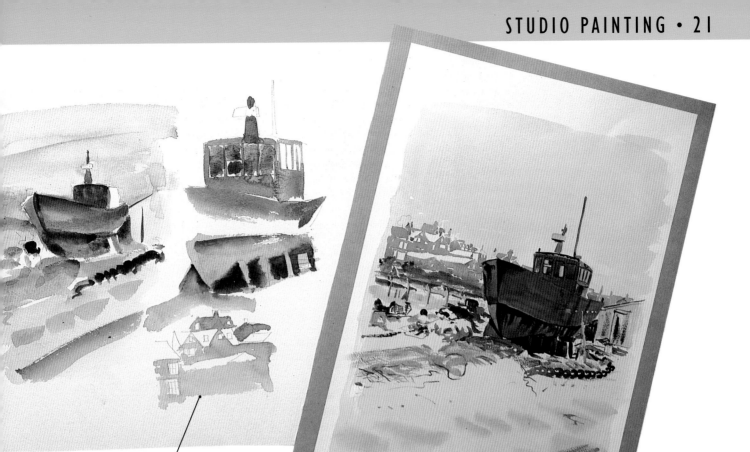

The color notes were also done on location, simply as a reference. Neither detail nor correct proportions were important in this case. Color notes can be in written form, but in this case the subtle hues were more accurately recorded with watercolor.

The final painting, done in the studio, is a natural progression of the previous references. Although the visual reference played a major role, the painting was done soon after, and visual memory and knowledge of the scene also played a part.

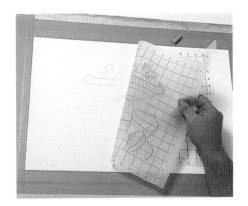

3 **When the drawing is completed, rub over the back of the trace with colored chalk, under the drawn lines. Tape the trace in place on the watercolor paper, chalk side down, and redraw over the existing drawing; the lines will be transferred to the paper in the form of chalk marks. Remove the trace.**

Scaling up a rectangle

An integral part of squaring up is the enlargement of a rectangle, which can be done quickly and simply, without the need for calculations. This will ensure that the shape used for the finished painting is exactly the same proportion as the sketch or photograph. The same method can be used to reduce a rectangle, though this is less common. You will need a set square, a ruler, a pencil, the original reference and a sheet of tracing paper, which is taped over the original. First draw the bottom line, then the left vertical line. This forms the bottom left corner shared by the original and the enlargement.

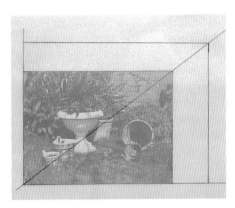

Place the reference in this corner and draw a diagonal line through the bottom left corner and the top right corner of the original. Continue this line extending to the top right. At any point on this line you can drop a vertical to the base line and a horizontal to the left-hand vertical. This will form your new scaled-up rectangle.

Color

Most colors have been standardized and you will see the same color names occurring in different brands as well as other painting media. This makes it easier if you are unable to obtain a color in your usual brand. There are more than 80 colors, but you need only a fraction of these to get you started; I have suggested 15, from which you can mix all the necessary colors.

Each color has different physical properties, which you need to understand, as it will affect the way you mix and use them. Some colors are very concentrated and you need only small amounts, otherwise they overpower other colors on the palette. These strong colors tend to be the dyes like alizarin crimson and phthalocyanine blue. Others are granular, leaving grainy textures, but are less intense in hue.

Watercolors obey all the same color laws as other media, but there is one important difference, in that watercolor is transparent. Instead of adding white to make a color paler, you add more water, causing greater fluidity. The color of the paper, usually white but occasionally tinted, plays an intrinsic part, because the colors laid on it are transparent glazes that allow the paper to show through. These two pages and those that follow, which explore some of watercolor's unique properties, will help you to understand and appreciate this attractive medium.

The primary color wheel

A little knowledge of basic color theory is essential for the aspiring artist, and will help you learn to mix colors successfully. The three primary colors – red, yellow, and blue – are those that cannot be mixed from any other color. These are the foundation stones of color. From these you can mix the three secondary colors – orange, green, and purple – then the three tertiaries (mixtures of three colors) and so on. In theory you can mix all colors from the primaries.

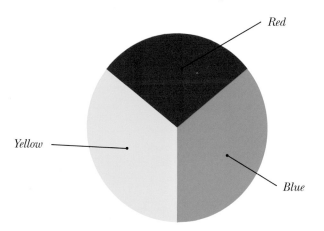

Red

Yellow

Blue

Warm colors

Not all primary colors are the same; there are different reds, blues, and yellows. A very helpful distinction to make is the color "temperature." In the overall color spectrum, red and yellow can be described as "warm" colors and at the other end, blue and purple as "cool." The same distinction can be made within each color group, albeit more subtly. Shown in the color wheel below are warm versions of the primary colors, with the secondary colors produced by mixing them.

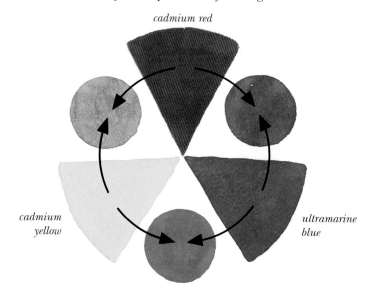

cadmium red

cadmium yellow

ultramarine blue

Cool colors

The primary colors below are the cooler versions. For example, the yellow has no red in it and veers to the green. The red has no yellow in it and veers to the purple, while the blue has no red content and veers to the green. The secondaries produced when these are mixed are different from their counterparts above.

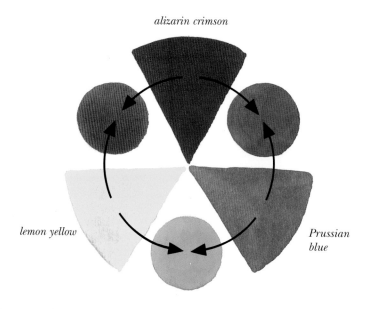

alizarin crimson

lemon yellow

Prussian blue

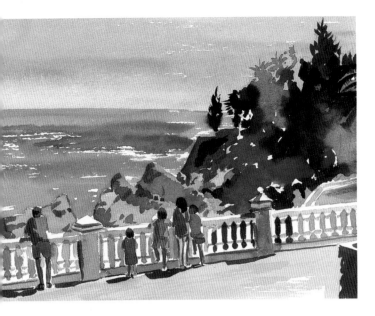

▲ This painting was produced by using a limited palette of the three warm primary colors in the color wheel shown left. Compare it with the cool version of the same painting, and you will see noticeable differences. The red clothes are much warmer and so is the ultramarine sky. The overall warmth of the colors suits the subject matter well.

▲ In this version, made with the cool primaries, there is a definite shift in the color spectrum. In some areas it is very obvious, for example the greens are cooler and fresher, as lemon yellow mixed with any blues will produce bright greens. The Prussian blue sea has a greener cast to it.

Suggested palette

Warm and cool versions of the primaries are essential, plus some secondaries and some of the so called "earth colors." The latter may seem rather nondescript to the beginner, but they are of vital importance, because they are close to many of nature's colors. Black is not included, but can be a good addition as it is more or less impossible to produce by mixing other colors. Other useful but not strictly essential colors are raw umber and indigo.

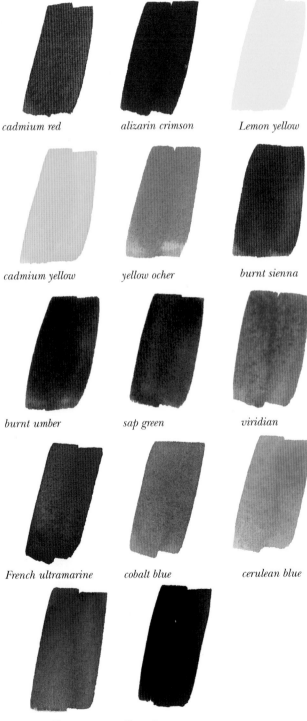

cadmium red — alizarin crimson — Lemon yellow

cadmium yellow — yellow ocher — burnt sienna

burnt umber — sap green — viridian

French ultramarine — cobalt blue — cerulean blue

Prussian blue — Payne's gray

Lighter drying

Watercolors look darker when wet than when dry, so you may find that a wash is less intense than you thought. You can compensate by laying a secondary wash over the first when it has dried, but it is wiser to try out a mixture on a spare piece of paper first. The example right clearly shows the righthand wet brushstroke is darker than the dry one on the left.

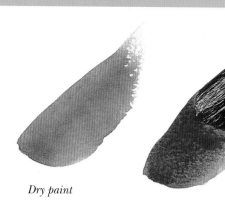

Dry paint

Wet paint

Concentrated red with a little water

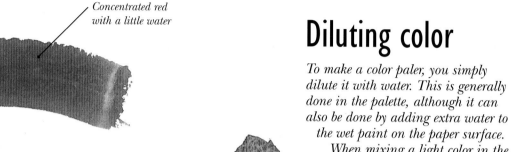

Diluting color

To make a color paler, you simply dilute it with water. This is generally done in the palette, although it can also be done by adding extra water to the wet paint on the paper surface. When mixing a light color in the palette, add water progressively with a wet brush or dropper, then mix it in well. With experience you will be able to judge at this stage how it will appear, but a large amount of wet paint can look misleadingly dark, so again make sure of the dilution by making swatches on paper.

Double the water content

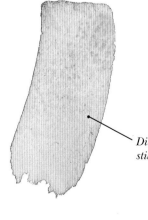

Diluted still further

Granulation

Some pigments are dyes that stain the paper, but others have sedimentary qualities, and as they dry, they settle into granular textures. When you begin painting this may not seem desirable, but once this characteristic is understood it can be utilized to create interesting effects. Manganese blue is one of the most granular, followed by cobalt blue, ultramarine blue, and the earth colors. The effect can be enhanced by mixing some of these colors together.

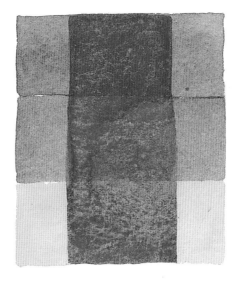

▲ A vertical strip of manganese blue has been painted over horizontal strips of alizarin crimson, viridian, and cadmium yellow. The granulation of the blue allows the bright undercolors to show through, highlighting the grainy texture.

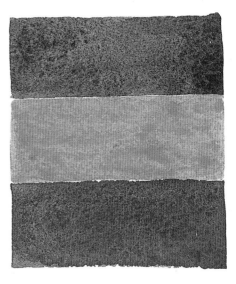

▲ Manganese blue is mixed with (from top) burnt umber, cadmium yellow, and burnt sienna. Interesting effects are created, because although the two colors do mix, the blue still separates out.

Different mixing methods

If two colors are mixed together in the palette, the resulting mixture will be an even, flat color with its properties already determined. But when two colors are mixed wet, on the paper surface, they blend more erratically, producing exciting effects. You can brush them together thoroughly or allow the water to blend them together. Both mixing methods are commonly integrated into one painting.

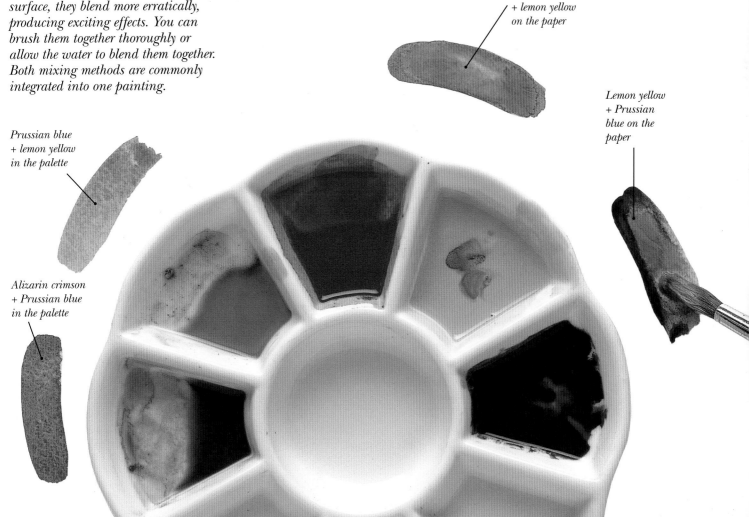

Alizarin crimson + lemon yellow on the paper

Lemon yellow + Prussian blue on the paper

Prussian blue + lemon yellow in the palette

Alizarin crimson + Prussian blue in the palette

Two-color mixes

At the outer edges of this chart are the 14 colors in the suggested starter palette, seven running down the lefthand side and seven along the top. The squares show the colors mixed together in equal proportions. Further variations can be made by altering the proportions or adding more water.

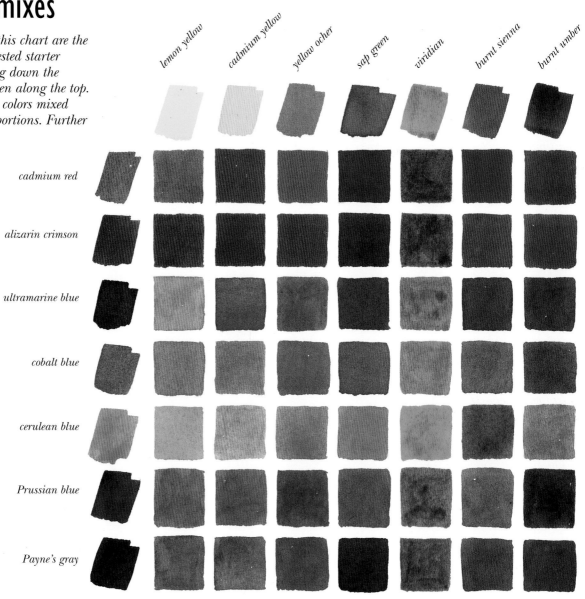

lemon yellow   cadmium yellow   yellow ocher   sap green   viridian   burnt sienna   burnt umber

cadmium red

alizarin crimson

ultramarine blue

cobalt blue

cerulean blue

Prussian blue

Payne's gray

Three-color mixes

When the three primary colors are mixed together they have the effect of cancelling each other out, producing a neutral gray. By using more of one color than another you can give the neutral a more distinctive bias, for example a warm or cool gray, or various shades of brownish gray. It is important to understand how to mix these neutral colors without producing muddy hues as many subtle nuances of color are found in nature.

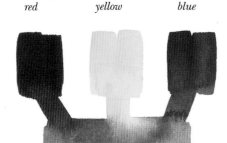

cadmium red	cadmium yellow	ultramarine blue

▲ *The three warm primary colors are mixed together equally to produce a warm gray.*

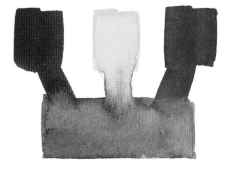

alizarin crimson	lemon yellow	Prussian blue

▲ *The three primary colors are mixed together to produce a cool gray.*

Overlaying two colors

Because watercolor is transparent you can mix colors on the paper surface by laying one over another. This can create a fresher, more vibrant effect than pre-mixing in the palette. Overpainting colors has to be done carefully in one stroke, to avoid disturbing the undercolor.

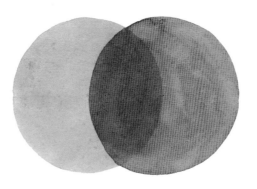

cerulean blue   *alizarin crimson*

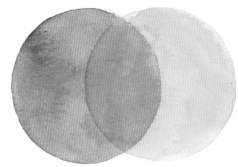

violet   *lemon yellow*

Overlaying three colors

These examples show the overlaying of first two colors and then three – where all three circles meet. Subtle color mixes can be achieved, which may have a bias to the more dominant color. The lefthand mixtures, for example, are dominated by the alizarin crimson.

alizarin crimson

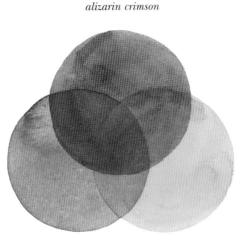

ultramarine blue   *cadmium yellow*

cadmium orange

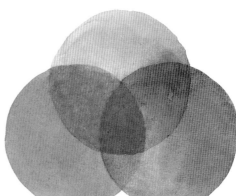

viridian   *alizarin crimson*

Transparency

Some colors are less transparent than others. Here swatches of all the colors of the suggested palette have been painted over a bar of ultramarine to demonstrate this. Pigments are derived from different sources, either organic or inorganic, and they have different properties which affect their transparency. The sedimentary colors like burnt umber, for example, tend to be slightly opaque, while the staining colors such as alizarin crimson are very transparent.

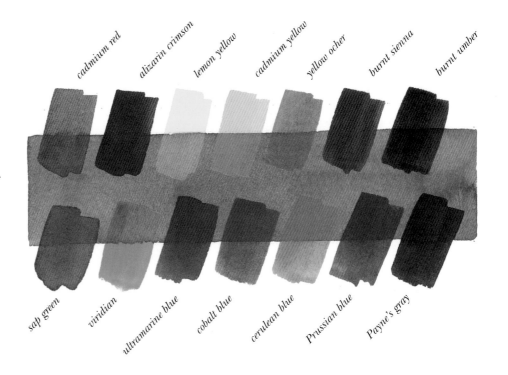

cadmium red   *alizarin crimson*   *lemon yellow*   *cadmium yellow*   *yellow ocher*   *burnt sienna*   *burnt umber*

sap green   *viridian*   *ultramarine blue*   *cobalt blue*   *cerulean blue*   *Prussian blue*   *Payne's gray*

Making corrections

As a general rule it is best not to tamper with a finished watercolor painting because you will disturb the delicate washes, and there is a danger of overworking. But inevitably mistakes are made, or you may want to add or remove parts of the composition. If you have worked up a painting from sketches, serious mistakes are less likely, due to the prior planning. But when you paint directly from life, in a rush to get it all down, you can make wrong decisions, which become glaringly obvious back at the studio. The popular belief that once it's down on paper it's too late is far from true; there are several ways to make corrections and remain discreet. Any correction that involves adding darker paint is quite straightforward, but otherwise you will have to get back to the white paper by removing paint. Another alternative is to use body color to paint over the mistake.

Lifting off freehand

Large areas can be scrubbed with a wet bristle brush and then dabbed with tissue to remove color. This method should be restricted to quality heavyweight paper or stretched paper. Don't try it on cartridge paper, which will fur up with rubbing.

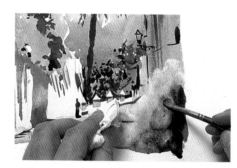

2 With a folded tissue in one hand and a bristle brush in the other, apply fresh water with the brush and scrub the dark paint until it dissolves, then dab and soak it up with the tissue. Apply more fresh water and repeat until most or all of the dark paint is removed.

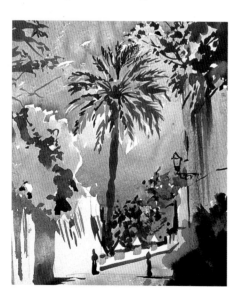

1 The painting is marred by the ugly mass of bushes at bottom right, which seems out of place, blocking the view down the street. It is decided to remove this.

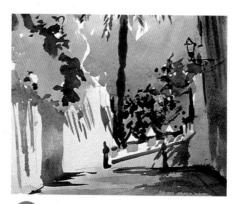

3 The paper will be slightly roughened by the scrubbing, but this causes no problem. The offending bush has completely disappeared, leaving no sign, and the righthand wall, road, and blue shadow has been painted in its place.

Acetate

Before you attack your painting with serious alterations, it's a good idea to preview them first. You can buy clear acetate designed to accept paint from graphic suppliers. You can lay this over the painting, and paint on it. It will have a slightly different finish to it, appearing slightly blotchy, but you will get a good idea of how the correction will appear.

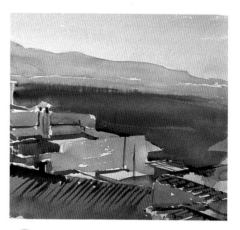

1 The painting looks a bit bland. Painting a row of trees beyond the houses would give it more punch, but without planning the painting could be spoiled.

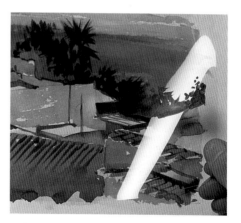

2 Acetate is laid over the painting, hinged at the top with masking tape, and the trees painted on. It is best to thicken the paint slightly with a little gum arabic, as the acetate has a slippery surface. If the first attempt fails you can start again with another sheet of acetate until you are satisfied, and then proceed to the painting itself, copying from the acetate.

Masking and lifting off

If you decide to add something geometric like the sail of a yacht or roof of a barn you can cut it out of masking tape, then scrub with a bristle brush and dab off with tissue. The making tape must not be removed until the paper has dried, otherwise it will tear. Then you can paint into the white space you have made. There is not much wrong with this painting in this sequence, but it could benefit from the addition of an extra foreground element, and it is decided to introduce a barn coming in from the right.

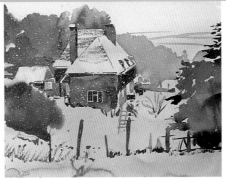

1 The roof is a lighter color, so some of the dark tree will need to be removed. The roof shape has sharp edges, so two strips of masking tape are used, and the curved edges are cut with a scalpel.

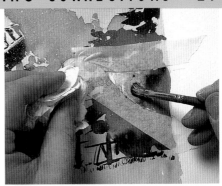

2 The inside edge of the masking tape must be pressed down firmly to create a watertight seal. Load a bristle brush with water and scrub out the paint, soaking it up with a tissue held in the other hand. Work right up to the masking tape.

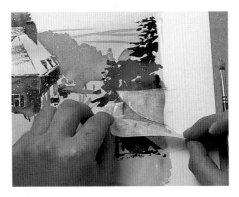

3 Leave to dry. Then peel back the tape, ensuring that it does not lift any paper. If this happens, use the scalpel to separate the tape and paper with a little incision under the peeled-back tape.

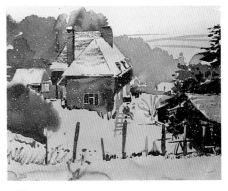

4 Once the tape is removed, you can paint in the roof, complete the barn's outline, and spray on a little body color as snow.

Using body color

In some circumstances, for example if the paper is too thin to take too much scrubbing, or if the dye in the pigment has stained the paper, you can resort to body color to cover over the mistakes. In this painting the two main elements are close together, requiring something placed in the foreground. Another plum is an obvious choice, but it will need bright highlights.

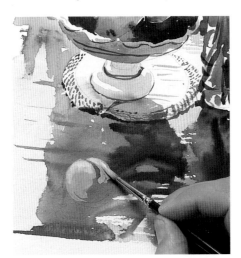

1 White body color (gouache) is mixed with a little blue and the lighter side of the plum is painted in. The highlighted edge is built up with a few layers of progressively purer white.

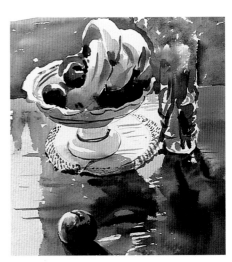

2 Ordinary watercolor, thickened with a little gum arabic, is used to paint the rest of the plum. Using body color in only one area can create an uneasy effect, but here it works well.

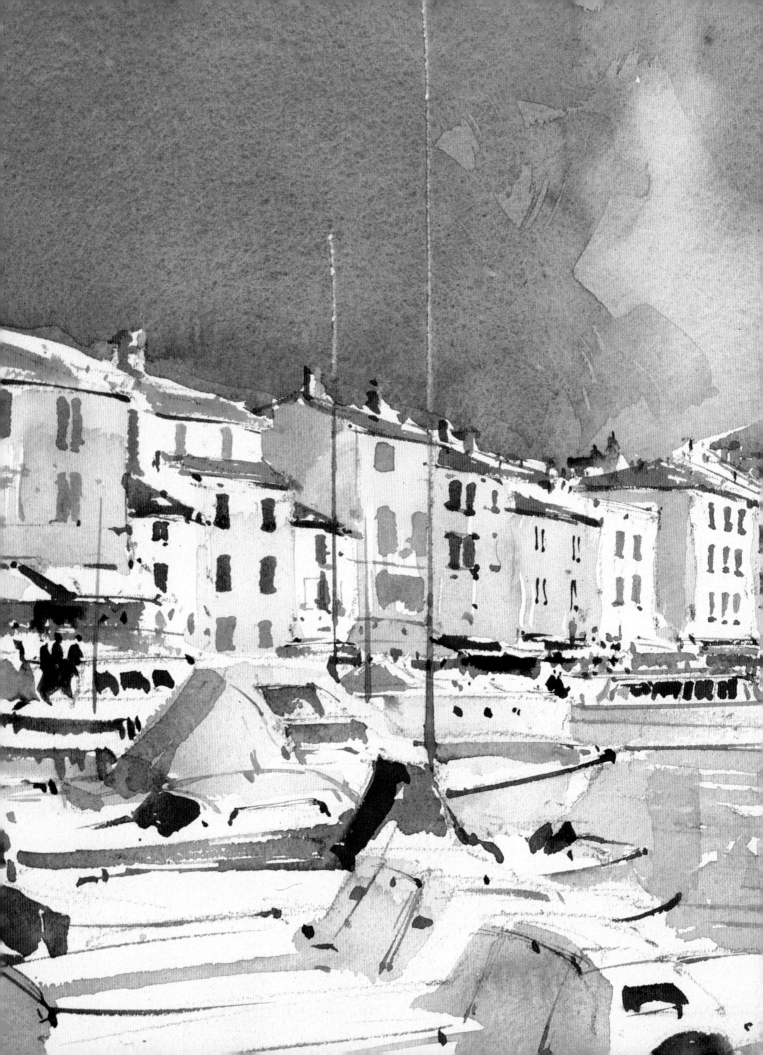

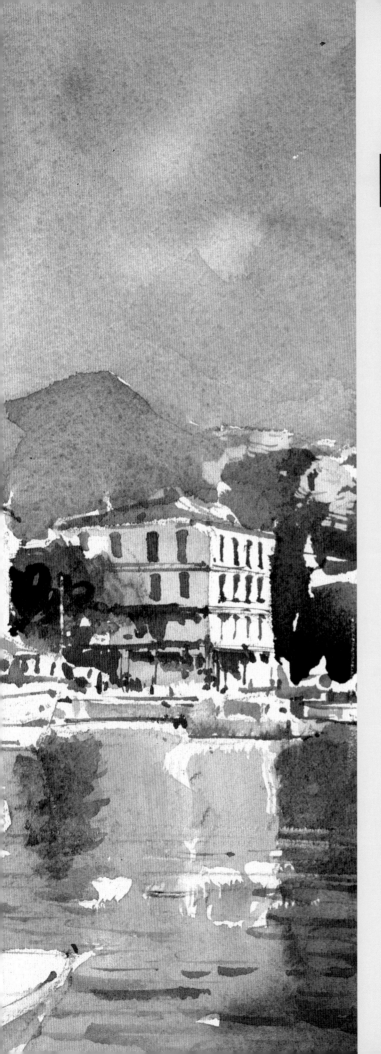

BASIC TECHNIQUES

The watercolor artist has a huge range of techniques to call on ranging from perfectly laid washes to scratched back highlights. In this section we look at the basic techniques available to the artist. Each technique is demonstrated with step-by-step sequences showing its application for a variety of subjects. The demonstrations are backed up by specially chosen and carefully annotated finished paintings which enable you to see how individual artists have adapted the methods to suit their subjects.

Cassis Harbor, Provence
Alan Oliver

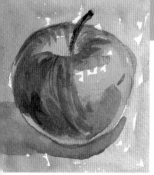

Small washes are the building blocks of a painting and may be no bigger than an individual brushstroke. You can use them individually to describe shapes or apply them collectively to build up a complex picture. You can also overlap them to build up tones and enrich colors, or interlock them like a jigsaw. They may be geometric and precise in shape or comprise irregular and free-flowing forms.

Interlocking flat washes

This painting is done with a progressive build-up of paint, from large to small areas, which collectively read as a group of three-dimensional objects. The interplay of lights and darks and interesting patterns all play an integral part. Draw the ellipses and curves with special care, as these make up the bulk of the shapes.

Small flat wash

After you have outlined the shape in pencil, you can either dampen the paper or leave it dry. As you begin painting onto a damp surface, bear in mind that the paint will spread quickly and erratically, creating soft furry edges – this is the fun of watercolor. If applied to a wet surface, the color will fade more as it dries. A dry surface offers more control and sharper edges. If you are butting up washes and do not want colors to intermingle, you should dry earlier washes first. You can speed the process up with a hairdryer.

1 **With a 1 inch (2.5cm) hake, lay a pale wash over the whole area, hinting at fluctuations in tone and color with light cadmium red, yellow ocher, indigo, and ultramarine. When dry, apply another overall wash, this time working around the palest objects.**

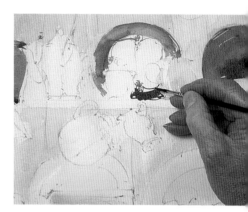

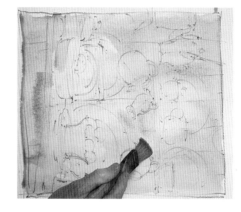

2 **When the washes are completely dry, use a medium brush to paint the objects on the top shelf, with ultramarine, indigo, permanent rose, and violet. Use a fine brush to paint the intricate patterns.**

VARIATION • 1
Overlaying flat washes

1 *This precise drawing matches the style of the rest of the painting with its pure, simple washes. Use a medium brush to paint the first washes of yellow gamboge, sap green, and a mixture of rose madder genuine and cobalt blue. Soften the highlight on the teapot while wet.*

2 *When completely dry, go over all the objects with smaller washes of the same colors, defining their darker tones. Use a pointed No. 2 brush for the smaller areas, carefully painting accurate ellipses in the saucers.*

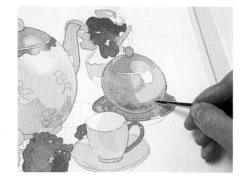

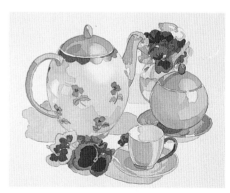

3 *Using very small washes, paint in all the decorative detail on the teapot and flower stamens. The limited palette used here is very effective in producing perfect color harmony, and the placement of the objects produces a well-balanced composition.*

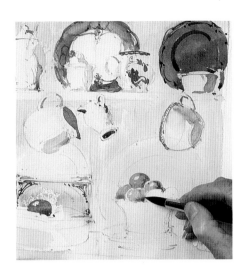

3 Reserving white paper for the lightest areas, paint the remaining objects with simple, flat washes. Paint the oranges with Indian yellow, dropping in a very small amount of alizarin crimson. Add a little detail with small understated touches.

5 This painting has been achieved almost entirely with simple flat washes, using very little wet-in-wet blending, except on the first wash. The result is delightfully fresh and bright, including exactly the right amount of detail and creating many exciting shapes and patterns to interest the eye.

4 Paint the shadows under the shelves and behind the objects in light red with a little indigo. They help to outline other objects with interlocking shapes.

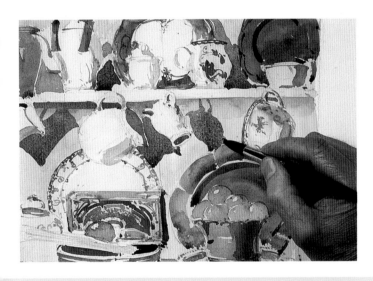

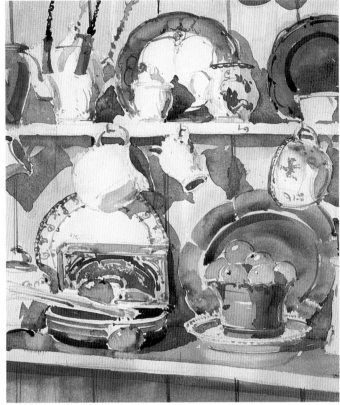

VARIATION • 2
Simple washes

1 *Paint the three main flower areas in alizarin crimson, ultramarine with Winsor violet, and cadmium yellow pale, using a No. 6 brush. Do this on a dry surface to retain crisp edges, but allow slight fluctuations of color within each object.*

2 *When dry, paint sepia on the red flower to separate the petals, Venetian red and crimson on the yellow, and concentrated ultramarine on the blue/violet flower. While these are drying, apply yellow to the center of each flower, allowing the colors to blend.*

3 *Paint the leaves and stalks in variations of cadmium yellow pale and ultramarine. These variations in color and tone prevent the plants appearing flat, and place them in a three-dimensional space.*

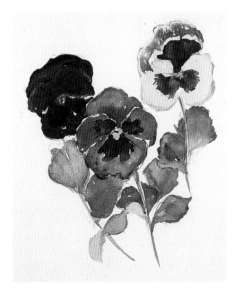

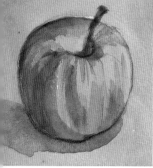

The fluidity and transparency of watercolor in a medium wash provides a foundation for further glazes and detail, enabling you to build up the painting with a series of washes like luminous veils. Working from light to dark in progressive layers creates an illusion of space as of overlapping objects in a landscape.

Luminous veils

A skilled artist is able to view a picture and break it down to a series of simple, flat washes. This is the key to watercolor painting, as you can then construct a picture methodically, the end result appearing complex and convincing, with the addition of a little detail to emphasize the point of interest. This painting builds up many subtle washes creating a soft atmospheric effect with minimum detail.

Medium flat wash

You can map out the early stages of a painting with several washes of different colors to divide the picture into distinct areas. This stage is important as it underpins subsequent painting. Begin by mixing sufficient paint on a palette using a No. 9 or 10 round or ½ inch (1cm) sable brush. After squeezing out enough pigment, you can work out the desired water to pigment ratio by gradually adding more water, stirring the mixture, then testing the color by dabbing it onto scrap paper.

1 Do a pencil drawing to divide the white paper into an arrangement of geometric shapes. Use diagonals to create linear perspective. With a No. 9 sable brush, wash cobalt blue onto the dry sky area, and over two windows. When dry, wash yellow ocher over the remaining white paper.

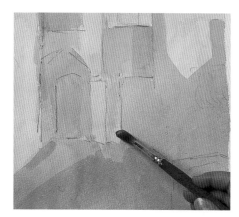

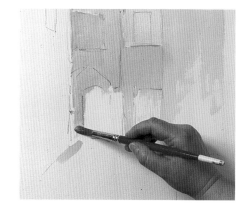

2 Paint a pale wash of Hooker's green around the top edge of the building, down the left corner, over the door, and continuing over the foreground. When dry, lay richer yellow ocher on the lower right wall and into the foreground, overlapping the green.

VARIATION • 1
Contrasting tones

1 *Clearly outline the different areas in pencil. Keep initial washes pale and of similar tone throughout. Use sap green for the palm leaf, burnt umber for the trunk, yellow ocher and burnt sienna for the walls, Payne's gray mixed with violet for the foreground sidewalk. Leave the parapet white.*

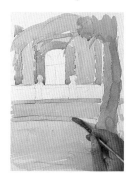

2 *The next set of washes should be significantly darker. Paint the leaf fronds with a mix of Payne's gray and sap green, and mix burnt sienna and violet for the shadows of the decorative brickwork. Use Payne's gray and burnt umber for the tree trunk. Add parapet detail in cerulean blue and the floor shadows in violet.*

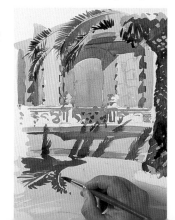

3 *Fill in with the final washes: burnt sienna on the brickwork and on the trunk, sap green and Payne's gray in the leaves, violet in the window. Paint the shaded leaf fronds and the window ironwork in Payne's gray. To finish, paint the fine brickwork detail in burnt sienna with a rigger.*

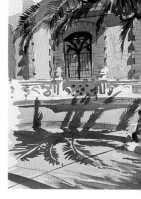

3 Apply combinations of burnt sienna and olive green to pick out the windows, doors, and areas of shadow. These washes should be darker and painted with greater fluidity. You will now have formed a clear distinction between the sunny upper half of the picture and the shaded lower- and foreground areas of the picture.

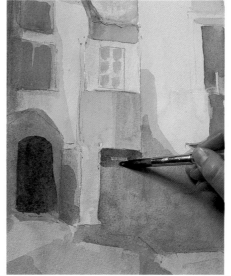

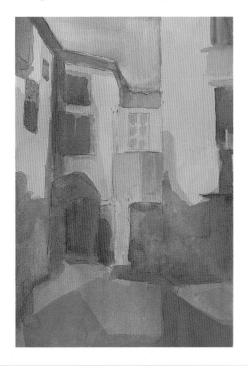

4 Apply subsequent washes, making them smaller and darker with more detail. Paint doors, window panes, balcony, and bars in Payne's gray. Wash Payne's gray mixed with ultramarine over the immediate foreground and bottom right retaining wall.

5 Underpaint the shrubbery with olive green and finish with pure viridian in loose brush-strokes to add a splash of bright color amidst a predominantly muted, earthy palette. Finally, use concentrated Payne's gray to bring the balcony railings and left window bars into sharp focus.

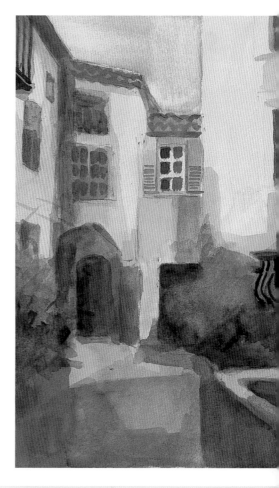

VARIATION • 2
Variable washes

1 *No drawing is done for this painting. Lay several adjacent washes and allow the colors to mingle where they meet. Use cerulean blue for the distant mountains, then monestial green for the middle distance, and finally yellow ocher, raw umber, and burnt sienna in the foreground.*

2 *Work fairly fast, applying the next wash before the previous one has dried. Apply a pale wash of cerulean blue for the sky, a second wash of monestial green in the middle ground, and Naples yellow in the foreground. Paint the fence in Prussian blue.*

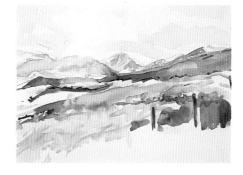

3 *Add detail to the mountains using more concentrated cerulean blue. Brush Prussian blue mixed with yellow ocher across the middle, then apply it in small dabs to suggest rough vegetation. The result is a loose, almost abstract painting that uses an exciting range of brushwork.*

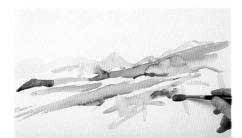

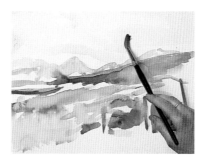

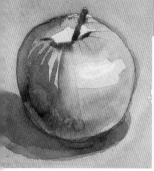

A large flat wash applied skillfully looks surprisingly fresh and luminous but is deceptively tricky to get right, requiring practice using different brushes, paper, and dilutions. This type of wash acts as a background or underpainting to be worked into whilst wet or dry. Part of an almost finished painting can also be skimmed over with a wash to soften and unify the underlying image, for example, if you wanted to throw a whole section into shade.

Assorted flat washes

In most paintings, you can use the full range of washes, which means that you will also need a range of brushes. A 1 inch (2.5cm) wash brush will usually suffice for the larger washes. For fine detail, a rigger or No. 0 brush is suitable, and for in-between work a round No. 10 with a good point will do. When splayed, this will cope with medium/large areas, and you can also draw the tip to a point for finer work.

Large flat wash

Watercolor is naturally a fast medium to use, but you should not rush into the painting. It is easy to underestimate the amount of paint needed so you will need to mix enough paint before you start, and use a heavyweight or stretched paper that will not buckle. A large mop brush, 1 inch (2.5cm) flat or similar, is best. Some decorator's brushes would do and a sponge works very well. Working reasonably fast with the board tilted slightly toward you, load your brush and with sideways strokes go back and forth across the page. Overlap each stroke slightly to pick up any excess fluid and to prevent a hard edge from forming. As soon as you finish the wash, lay the board flat to dry so that ripples do not form.

1 Use a 1 inch (2.5cm) hake to paint the sky with a broad wash of ultramarine, permanent rose, and yellow ocher. Mix cerulean blue with burnt umber and ultramarine for the trees and their reflections in the water. Use yellow ocher and permanent rose for the reflections of the buildings.

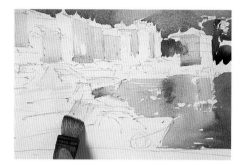

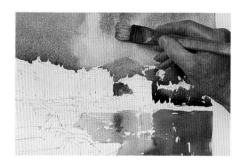

2 Using the flat edge of the hake, paint the buildings with pale washes of yellow ocher with a little permanent rose. Continue onto the boats, picking out all the small areas of color. Leave plenty of white paper to represent the sun's glare on this Mediterranean harbor scene.

VARIATION • 1
Large flat washes

1 *Using a 2B pencil, sketch in the room. Pay careful attention to perspective. When you are happy with the drawing, use cobalt blue and a fairly large, round brush for the first wash. Leave it to dry.*

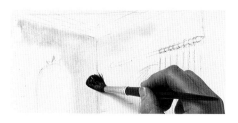

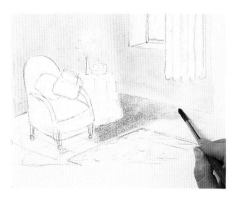

2 *Paint the floor with a mix of cerulean blue and a little Payne's gray. Carefully follow the outline, and keep the tone even throughout.*

3 *The right-hand wall is a darker tone because the light from the window is falling on the left-hand wall, so give it a second wash of cobalt blue. Mix enough paint initially and work fairly fast so that no hard edges form.*

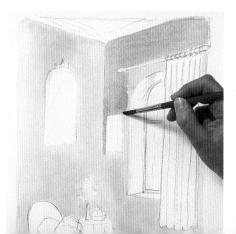

3 Using a No. 0 brush and a mix of cadmium red and Indian yellow, paint the roofs. Leave small areas of white paper, particularly against the purple sky, to "lift" the roofs making them appear brighter as they catch the sunlight.

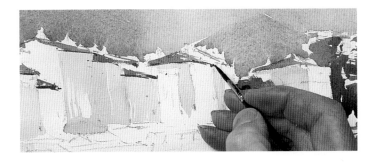

5 For the very tall masts, you'll need a mahl stick to steady your hand and achieve a straight line. A homemade one is shown here. Use a sharp blade to scrape out a line against the dark sky. Continue the line against the pale buildings using the point of the brush.

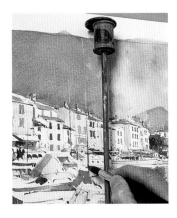

6 Apply a second flat wash to the left side of the sky to contrast with the pale buildings. The finished painting demonstrates a judicious use of white paper with only a few skillful touches to describe the shapes. The dark trees on the right direct the eye to the activity on the left.

4 Using the same brush, paint in all the windows. Don't try to make them perfectly rectangular, and vary the colors to add interest. You can also suggest activity with simple brushstrokes along the quay side to indicate people, cafés, and shops.

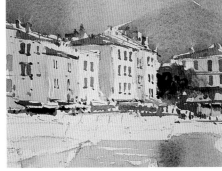

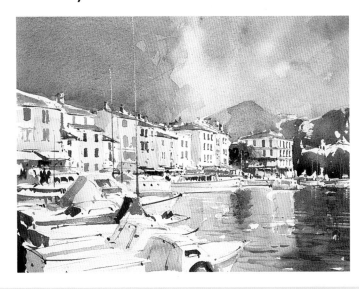

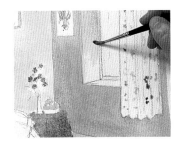

4 *Paint the side table in rose madder genuine. Mix that with cobalt blue for the fine detail on the curtains and the flowers. Once the wall has dried, you can paint the inside of the window with cobalt blue.*

5 *Paint the armchair with a flat wash of carmine, omitting the legs and cushions. Use carmine fairly thickly for the patterns on the rug, to leave texture resembling the carpet weave.*

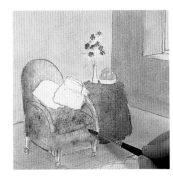

6 *Paint a second wash on the shaded part of the chair and add the detail of the corner of ceiling. Paint the cushions in yellow ocher. Do the folds for the tablecloth in the same color as before. Paint shadows with ultramarine and Payne's gray.*

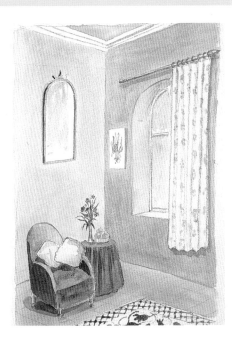

In context

These three paintings demonstrate a wide variety of sizes of wash. Each picture incorporates washes that fulfill different functions from decoration to basic picture construction. In each painting the washes comprise the major part, with a little detail and texture added at the end. The careful juxtaposition of lights and darks and varying concentrations of pigment in the washes in "Rooftops, Clovelly" and "Coffee Break" produce the evocative atmospheric effects of these two paintings.

Rooftops, Clovelly

Tom Groom

Three distinctly different kinds of washes are used in this painting. Each exploits the paper surface in a different way. Depth is achieved by gradually reducing the concentrations of paint on the rooftops toward the horizon. The warm underpainting in the middle distance, keeps the attention focused in the center of the painting.

The sea is a large pale wash. This was painted carefully, outlining the rooftops and chimneys.

The first wash to be applied was this pale yellow and pink, which is allowed to show between the rooftops.

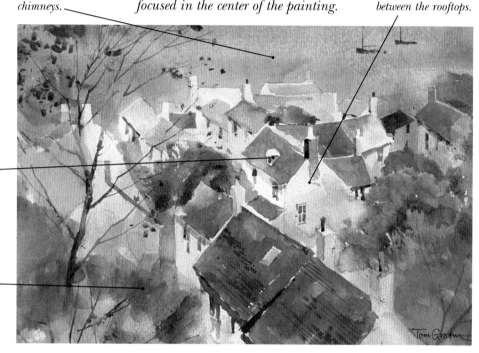

The rooftops range from medium to small rectangular washes, painted accurately and converging into the distance. These are all painted over a pale background wash.

The trees and shrubery are loosely painted washes, incorporating some dry-brush for texture.

Coffee Break

Karen Mathis

This painting is almost entirely constructed from washes. It is a good example of how flat washes can be overlaid to build up richness and depth of color. This kind of brilliance can be achieved only with several "veils" of color and a good understanding of the effect of the initial yellow wash.

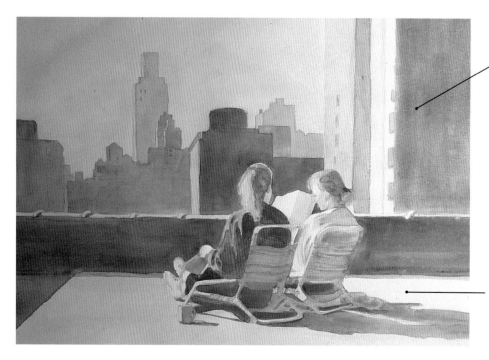

Up to five washes were overlaid, showing a predominance of cobalt blue to contrast with the warm yellow sky.

A bright yellow wash was applied over the whole picture area, with the exception of a few highlights on the figures. The wash is at its palest in the foreground.

Garden Poppies

Maurice Read

In this painting the overlaying of paint is kept to a minimum in order to preserve the freshness of each wash. The juxtaposition of lights and darks creates a lively counterpoint between the undulating shapes of the flowers and foliage. The shape of each wash plays a descriptive role, therefore little detail is needed in order to complete the painting.

Simple flat washes were painted into which further paint was added into both wet and dry surfaces to create texture and to suggest detail.

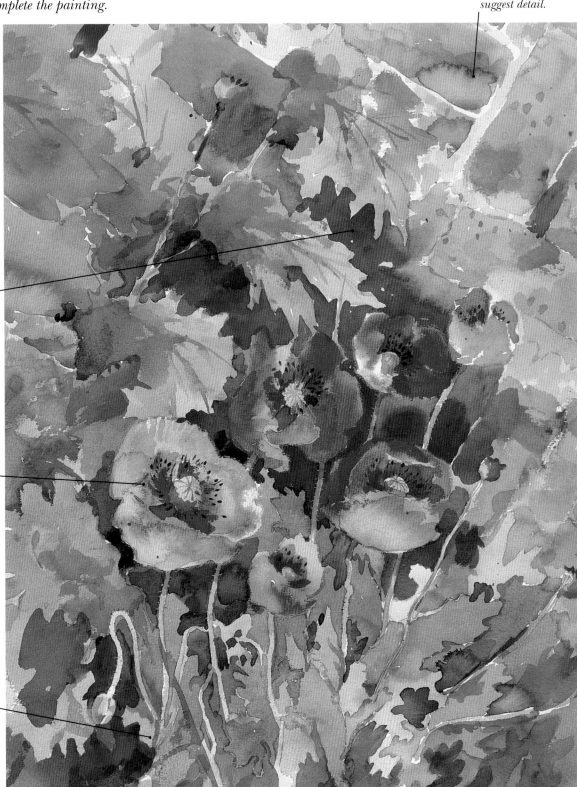

Freehand undulating shapes were skillfully painted in burnt sienna to describe the leaf shapes, create shadow, and to provide contrast with the pale green leaves.

The details of the flower centers were painted in a pale pink wash, into which further colors were added wet-in-wet to create interesting backruns and special effects.

Washes were overlaid to create a complex pattern of almost abstract shapes that act as a perfect stage for the bright red flowers. The colors of the bottom half of the picture are predominantly cool to emphasize the red petals.

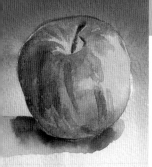

From the gentle gradations in the sky to the varying colors in the skin of an apple, subtle changes in tone and color are all around us, so the ability to capture them is important. The illusive medium of watercolor must be properly controlled because you only get one chance when applying a large area of wash.

Graded wash

To achieve a gradual, even reduction in tone, you should first lay down the darkest tone then systematically dilute the paint with each stroke by adding water. Having several premixed dilutions to hand will simplify this. You can progress from light to dark or vice-versa. It may be necessary to rework weak areas, adding or subtracting paint (see Lifting Out, page 94). You can do this immediately or wait until the paint is completely dry and go over it again. To blend two colors, premix both, paint one alongside the other, then paint one into the other with several strokes. From the mixing of the two colors, a third color will form.

Gradual transition of color

Plan and mix all the colors in advance. If you prepare sufficient paint, you won't need to wet the paper before painting because you'll be able to work fast enough to prevent any streaks forming. Working on dry paper in this way means that the colors will be more intense after they have dried. Apply masking fluid in the windows and for the sun's reflection on the water so that you can paint in wide, uninterrupted strokes across the picture.

1 Mask the windows with masking fluid. Then paint the sky, brushing a band of blue across the top, followed by yellow ocher, burnt sienna, and finally Payne's gray, blending each color with the one before. Take the colors across the outline of the building.

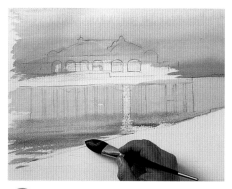

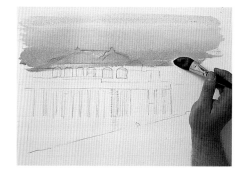

2 When the sky has dried, paint the sea in bands, beginning with yellow ocher, then cadmium red, and finally cobalt blue. (Mask out the sun's reflection first.) Use a dryer brush for the foreground blue in order to leave patches of white, then apply a few streaks of darker blue.

VARIATION · I
Single color

1 *Prepare enough fairly concentrated Antwerp blue on your palette and have some clean water available. Working from the top, paint backward and forward across the paper. As you progress down the paper, gradually add more water. Apply plenty of paint and work fast in order to achieve a smooth change of tone.*

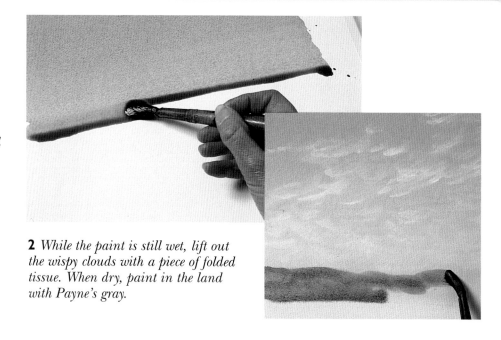

2 *While the paint is still wet, lift out the wispy clouds with a piece of folded tissue. When dry, paint in the land with Payne's gray.*

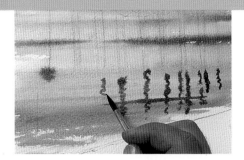

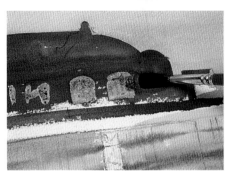

3 While the sea is still wet, paint in streaks of cadmium red. When it is just damp, paint in the reflections of the pier supports with black, wiggly lines. When those are almost dry, apply some horizontal black strokes over them.

4 Using a No. 10 brush, paint in the pier with Prussian blue, omitting a few patches for chinks of light along the bottom. Paint the beach with Prussian blue, adding black in parts. Leave tiny chinks of white paper to suggest light hitting odd pebbles.

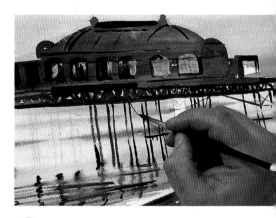

5 When dry, use a No. 4 brush and black paint to suggest the detail on the pier. Continue painting the upright supports, varying the thickness of these lines. Use a little dry-brush in areas to show the play of light flickering on the corroded metal.

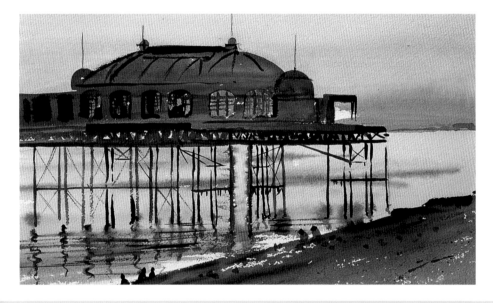

6 Remove the masking fluid and with Venetian red paint the windows. When dry, use black to paint the window frames. Use cadmium yellow and red to paint the sun's reflections on the water. Finally, paint a few red dry-brush strokes horizontally and away from the reflections.

VARIATION • 2
Double overlaid wash

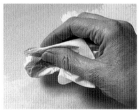

1 *Turn the board upside down and paint a graded wash of well-diluted alizarin crimson, remembering to dampen the paper slightly first to prevent streaking. Then turn the board right way up and, when the red is dry, apply a graded wash of Antwerp blue.*

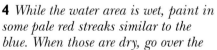

2 *While the blue is wet, dab out the clouds with crumpled kitchen paper to create a fluffy texture. Leave to dry. (To speed this up, you can use a hairdryer.)*

3 *Paint the land in two undulating, horizontal strips of pale alizarin crimson mixed with Antwerp blue. The second strip should be double the concentration of the first. When dry, re-wet the water area and drop in streaks of Antwerp blue.*

4 *While the water area is wet, paint in some pale red streaks similar to the blue. When those are dry, go over the area with a few more pale red horizontal strokes for the water ripples, increasing in intensity as they gradually recede.*

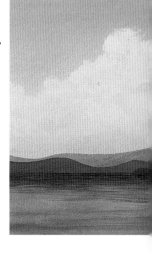

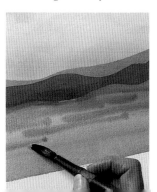

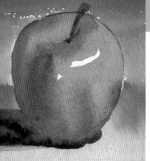

With careful observation, you will see that the world around us is multicolored. A rainbow or a sunset are typical examples of a series of colors merging one after the other. This is something you will want to reflect in your painting, and you can do this by utilizing watercolor's natural ability to blend one color with another.

Variegated wash

Many colors can be gently brushed on in a controlled way, or randomly dropped into a damp wash; the sponge-like paper will retain the dampness long enough for the different colors to seep into each other. The brushwork is only the first step – the rest is left up to the paint and paper. Don't use too much water as this will be too difficult to control and a lot of the pigment will drain away on drying. While the paint is drying, don't add more color or the gentle tones will be disrupted. Color mixing also occurs on the wet surface so keep your application fresh with limited but well-selected colors.

Variegated underpainting

Since this is a fairly large painting and the paper is pre-wet to accept the initial paint, you can use a medium decorator's brush or sponge to speed up the painting process. A damp rather than soaking surface is sufficient to accept paint, so squeeze out the brush or sponge and lift off any excess water. After you have dropped in the paint and it appears to have spread enough, use a hairdryer to arrest the process.

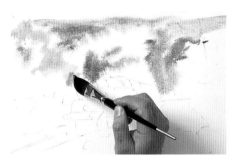

1 **Wet the whole surface with clean water, and drop in ultramarine and Payne's gray for the sky, cadmium yellow, terre verte, and sap green for the trees and foreground, and violet for the bluebells. Blot the foreground railtrack with kitchen paper to get back some white paper.**

2 **Allow these colors to bleed into one another and even partially bleed into the train area. The pencil lines should still be partially visible. Tilt the board toward you slightly and the colors will run downhill a little. When the blending is sufficient, speed up the drying with a hairdryer.**

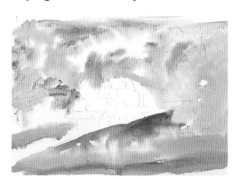

VARIATION • 1
Multicolored wash

1 *Wet the picture area with clean water, then paint in new gamboge in wide, horizontal brushstrokes, with the brush fully charged. Immediately follow this with bright red and alizarin crimson painted in some remaining white areas. Paint Antwerp blue in the white areas at top and bottom.*

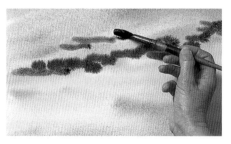

2 *Tilt the board at various angles to encourage the flow of paint in several directions. While the paint is still wet, drop in concentrated Payne's gray in wavy strips for cloud formations. Leave to dry.*

3 *Paint the distant horizon and water ripples with Payne's gray. This simple strip of paint effectively separates the water area from the sky, making sense of the previous washes and thus completing the painting.*

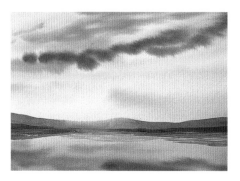

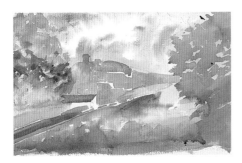

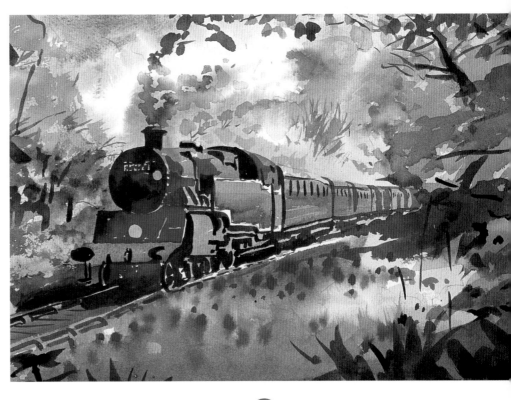

3 Do the underpainting for the train and railtrack with ultramarine, violet, Venetian red, and Hooker's green. Paint these in simple flat washes, allowing a little blending on the railtrack and rear carriages. Loosely suggest the midtones on the trees with a mix of sap green and Payne's gray.

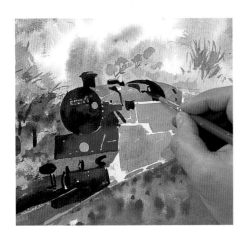

4 With a No. 5 brush, paint the darker areas and trunks of the trees. Dab ultramarine onto the foreground bluebell area, and spray on water with an atomizer to soften the effect. Use black and ultramarine to paint the dark detail on the train.

5 Finish off the rear of the train with a paler mix of colors. Paint the overhanging and foreground leaves in Payne's gray. Paint the railtrack in Payne's gray. Finally paint the smoke with diluted indigo.

VARIATION • 2
Small variegated washes

1 *With the two vegetables sketched in, lay a loose wash of Winsor yellow on the onion. While this is wet, add Venetian red and raw sienna with a little burnt umber around the edges, to suggest roundness.*

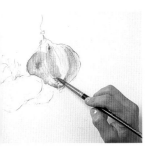

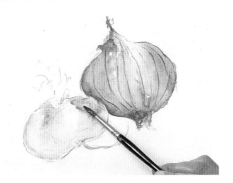

2 *When the onion has dried, use burnt umber to paint in the curved, vertical lines of the skin. Paint the turnip with an uneven wash of Naples yellow. While this is wet, drop cobalt violet onto the top half, and add into that a little raw sienna.*

3 *Wet the surrounding paper to allow the color to spread outside the turnip. While the turnip is still wet, paint the leaves with a variegated mix of Winsor yellow and ultramarine. This will run into the rest of the colors, leaving no hard edges.*

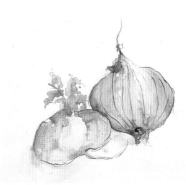

In context

Each example on these pages features the gradation or variation of washes in ways unique to watercolor. The washes are used skillfully to make clear statements evoking particular moods or weather conditions, as in "Maine Fishing Shanty" in which the artist has used an unusual and exciting vertical streaked effect to suggest torrential rain.

The streaked sky was produced by downward brushstrokes of paint applied to the wet surface of the background wash. The color was varied across the picture.

After the initial wash had dried, the roofs were reserved with masking fluid. The shapes of the roofs were subsequently defined by the next wash that was resisted by the mask. The only other definition is provided by the dark shadows under the eves.

Maine Fishing Shanty

Joan Combs Rudman

The variegated wash that is the key feature of this painting was applied first in several stages. Between stages selected parts, such as the central roof tops, were masked out. Apart from a few brushstrokes, suggesting doors, windows, telegraph poles, and other details, the variegated wash makes up the whole picture.

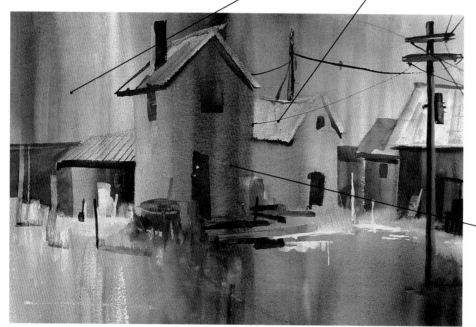

The buildings are composed of the same variegated wash, being distinguished from the background only by the addition of simple doors and windows. In this way they blend into the overall effect.

The sky has a slight, but very important gradated wash, which is a mirror image of the expanse of water and which it counterbalances. The dark clouds above have been added wet-in-wet to the wash.

Headland

Robert Tilling

The sheer simplicity of this painting belies its deftness and skill. The near perfect gradation of tone across the glassy water, could only have been achieved by a skillful application of the right amount of pigment to paper of optimum wetness, and with the minimum of brushwork. The impact of the finished work is stunning, as the eye is drawn to the eerie silhouette of the rocky pillar set against a luminously pale wash.

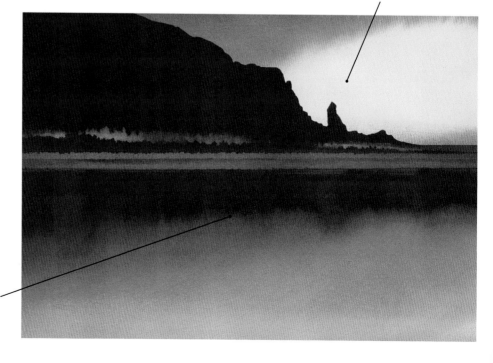

Much control was needed to create the hazy dark reflection of the mountains without losing the calmness of the water surface. The edges of the reflection are almost imperceptible.

The white disc of the sun was masked to retain the white paper. The halo was produced through careful blending of the surrounding wet wash, using a small brush.

The gradual transition from yellow to blue was achieved by painting the two bands of color side-by-side into a damp surface and merging them with horizontal strokes of a damp brush.

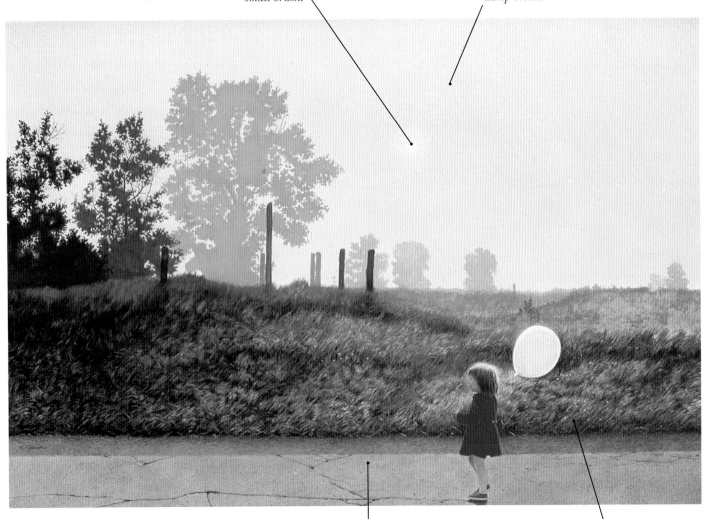

Morning Walk

Walter Garver

This gradated wash plays a crucial role in dictating the mood of this picture. The subtle transition of color across the sky, particularly around the sun, is the vital factor in the portrayal of the misty morning light. The top half of the picture is taken up with the sky and all the detail is confined to the bottom half. The silhouettes of the trees break up the sky area. The largest of these is closest to sky in color and tone.

A pale yellow wash was first applied as an underpainting, upon which the gray paint was brushed and spattered followed by the fine detail of the cracks in the surface. This gives the road a slight yellow bias, echoing the color of the sky.

The detailed grass was painted over an underpainting of bright yellow. The sense of yellow light permeating the whole scene is reinforced by the way in which the underpainting has been allowed to show through.

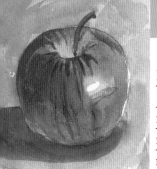

Painting on a dry surface is the most direct method, and the results are more predictable and dry more quickly. It's probably the best technique to start with, and you can progress to more difficult methods later. The brushstrokes are easily identifiable and the colors remain crisp and bright. Foreground images appear in sharp focus and you can add detail with a fine brush.

Wet-on-dry I

The wet-on-dry method is the foundation for other techniques such as glazing, since the surface must be dry to take further layers if you don't want them to mix. Brushmarks will stay fixed and not spread, so you can exploit the brush's full potential as a descriptive tool. Wet-on-dry techniques also allow you to outline contours to give them clear definition, and separate different planes and objects with sharp edges. If you want a soft edge, you can create this by running a wet brush along the edge before it dries. The entire sequence including initial wash, secondary glaze, object definition, and finishing touches can all be done wet-on-dry.

Wet-on-dry freshness

The method used here is to work on a dry surface, either clean paper or dry paint. The simple mixes, of usually not more than two colors at a time, and the variations of brushwork produce a painted surface which vibrates with the liveliness and freshness particular to watercolor. Additional techniques, such as spattering and knifing out, are discreetly applied to enhance the effect.

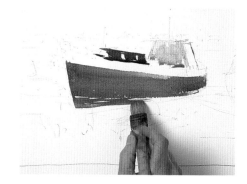

1 With Payne's gray and light red, and a 1 inch (2.5cm) hake, paint the hull of the boat. Paint the parts above the hull in light red, indigo, and violet.

2 Paint the foreground beach in burnt sienna with Payne's gray, and the red boxes in light red. Using a ¾ inch (1.9cm) decorator's brush, paint the background row of buildings in ultramarine.

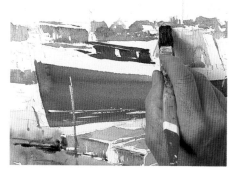

VARIATION • I
Geometric form with precise edges

1 *Apply separate washes of Indian yellow and cadmium scarlet for the wall, allowing them to mix on the surface. Use fairly concentrated violet and burnt sienna for the paving, also allowing them to mix. Use olive green for the foliage.*

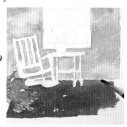

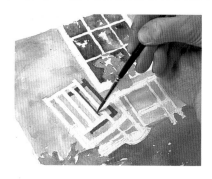

2 *Paint the window panes in Vandyke brown mixed with ultramarine, working in violet, burnt sienna, and olive green. Leave patches of white paper for reflections. Use a strong mix of Vandyke brown and a little cadmium scarlet for the table and chair shadows. Paint them with crisp edges.*

3 *Paint the flowerpots in burnt sienna. Wash the wall shadows in burnt sienna. Deepen the paving with a second wash of Winsor violet and ultramarine.*

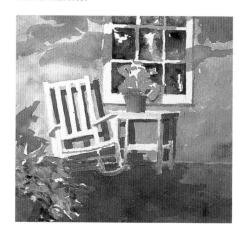

3 With the decorator's brush, spatter flecks of burnt sienna onto the beach. With a pointed brush, paint the mast with burnt sienna and a touch of ultramarine. Paint in the framework on the cabin with indigo.

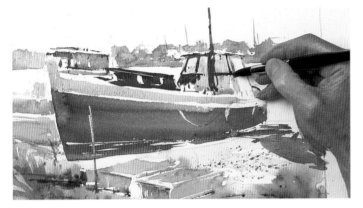

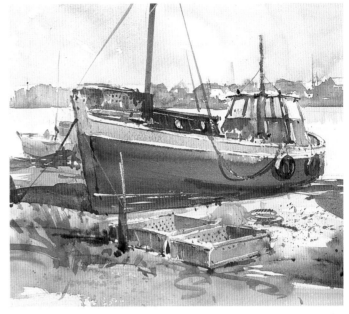

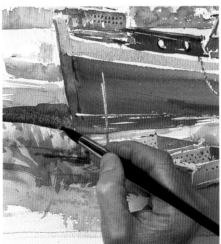

5 Do the mast and rigging with burnt sienna and a little cobalt blue. Then finish off all the smaller details with delicate touches applied with a fine brush.

4 Paint the sky with loose washes of ultramarine and cadmium red and yellow, allowing the colors to blend a little. Paint the buoy with concentrated cadmium yellow and a touch of cadmium red. For the dark cast shadow of the boat, use a mix of burnt sienna and ultramarine.

VARIATION • 2
Overlaying colors

I *Paint the oil lamp and the table beneath it with a wash of raw sienna. When dry, paint yellow ocher on the lamp top and base. Continue building up the distinctive metallic reflections with Vandyke brown.*

2 *Use olive green on the underside of the lamp, and Payne's gray with ultramarine for the cast shadow. With a much diluted wash of ultramarine, paint behind the lamp to kill the sharp contrast of white paper against it. Build up some darker tones on the top surface and around the neck. Using a fine brush and Vandyke brown, paint some thin, dark lines around the base and the wick hole. Then sharpen up some of the edges with the fine brush.*

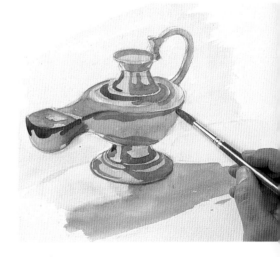

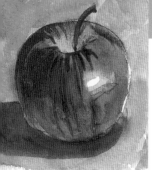

This is a versatile method, allowing both precise application and a loose, flowing technique incorporating a variety of individual brushstrokes. This Impressionistic approach results in splashes of exciting color showing vitality and energy, which can be complemented with a variety of textural brushstrokes. As a rule, it is advisable to maintain a balance between the dry and wet approaches.

Using specialized brushes

Painting onto a dry surface lends itself to a variety of brushmarks. For this picture, you will need a collection of brushes, each of which creates a different effect, providing the opportunity to produce a wide repertoire of brushmarks.

Wet-on-dry 2

Extreme wetness is restricted to a painterly approach. When working on dry paper, it's easier to control the concentrations of pigments and tonal variations. A dry paper can be exploited by using the rough surface texture to break up the brush strokes. This is more pronounced on cold-pressed papers. A large wash dries more quickly on dry paper, which, if painting outdoors, is a great advantage. As the paint dries there is less color lost than if painted into a wet surface.

① **Use a ¾ inch (1.9cm) decorator's brush and a mix of cadmium yellow and cobalt blue to paint the trees. Then paint the canopies using a mix of cadmium red, cadmium yellow, cobalt blue, and a little violet.**

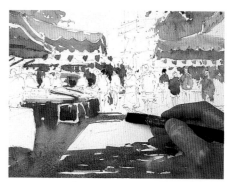

② **Using a smaller brush and a mixture of violet and a little burnt sienna, work around the picture, loosely picking out the large or small areas corresponding to that color, in the shaded parts under the canopies. Leave slivers of white paper between the areas of color to accentuate the sunlight.**

VARIATION • 1
Build-up of brushstrokes

1 *Start by painting the foreground garden with olive green and terre verte, the iron railing in a dark mix of ultramarine, permanent rose, and caput mortuum violet. Gradually build up the brushstrokes, leaving chinks of white paper.*

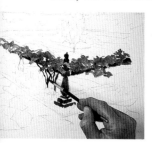

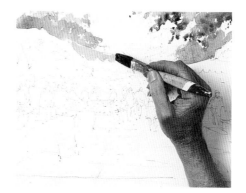

2 *Painting the dark, foreground tones first allows you to estimate the delicate mid and light tones and thus achieve the correct feeling of recession. Mix cerulean blue into the original green for the lower plants. Use Indian yellow, cadmium scarlet, Winsor violet, and ultramarine for the bright flowers.*

3 *Work progressively into the background, diluting the brushstrokes to build up the picture. Use a pale mix of burnt sienna and Winsor violet for the paving stones, and a darker mix for the cracks. Use a pale gray wash for the distant trees, and a pale neutral wash for the sky.*

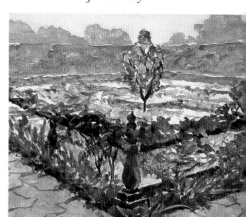

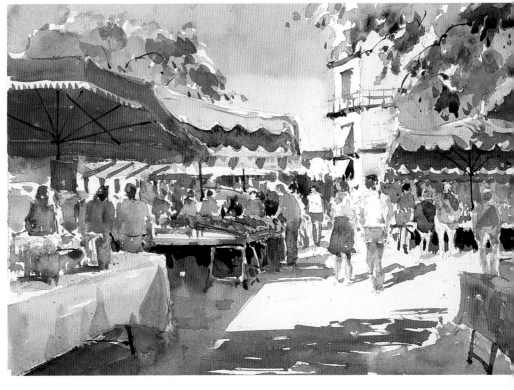

3 Use a pointed brush to suggest the detail with light brushstrokes. Paint the sky with a 1 inch (2.5cm) hake. Since it is not the lightest area, gauge its tone against the paler colors below.

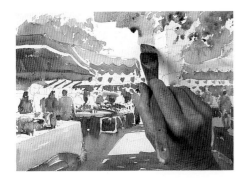

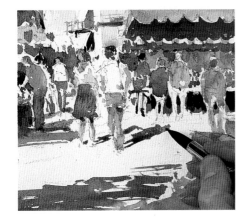

4 Continue to build up the picture, adding finer detail, with darker accents of color over existing washes, particularly indigo under the tables. Take advantage of specialized brushes to create variety with the paper grain, even with the smallest marks.

5 What looks like a complicated scene has been achieved quickly using a methodical approach. Much pencil work has been left visible in the reserved white areas, contributing to the busy effect. The immediacy of wet-on-dry and fresh colors ideally suits this lively picture.

VARIATION • 2
Wet-on-dry build-up

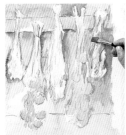

1 Use a ⅝ inch (1.6cm) flat brush to apply cadmium red and burnt umber background wash. Add a darker mix for the shadows. While wet, paint the wooden rail in burnt umber. Paint the flowers and leaves with cadmium yellow deep, Hooker's green, cadmium red, and cerulean blue.

2 Use sepia and a small, flat brush to build up dark, descriptive brushstrokes on the plants. Use sideways strokes to produce long, thin marks. Use a small, round brush for the dots.

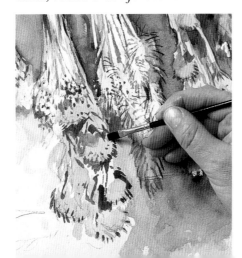

3 With sepia, darken the shadows around the plants to lift them away from the wall. The white paper showing through the plants emphasizes the variety of descriptive brushstrokes.

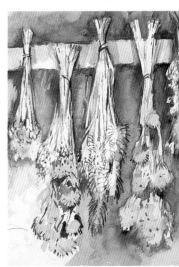

In context

A broad range of subjects can be tackled using the wet-on-dry method as is demonstrated by the three pictures shown here. Each painting incorporates fundamentally different approaches, reflecting the different style of each artist. Very little of watercolor's traditional fluidity is evident. In its place there is precision and detail; a further testament to the versatility of the medium.

After the Storm

Roy Preston

This is largely a painting of textures achieved by the direct application onto a dry surface. Fluid paint is visible only in the bottom grass area. The meticulous attention to detail and incorporation of special techniques like masking and scratching out makes this a highly exciting painting worthy of careful study.

Individual leaf shapes are defined by the dark green shadows painted over an initial green wash. Highlights have been added by lifting off.

The grass is painted with a fluid wash. During the drying process, various colors were added to produce a little blending. The tall grass stalks were painted with body color onto a dry surface.

The individual climber branches were painstakingly masked out with masking fluid applied with a fine brush. The roof was then painted with a broad wash.

The brick pointing was masked out with masking fluid, before washing over the bricks. Extra color has been added to various bricks at a later stage.

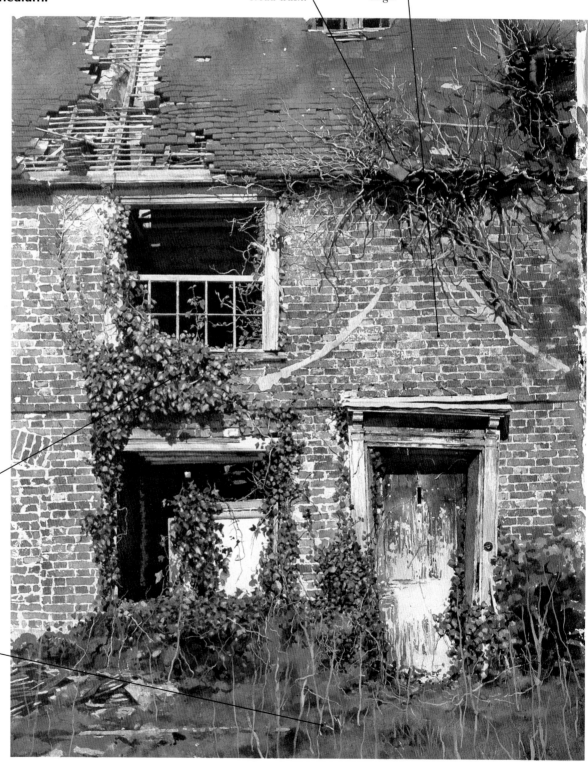

Beyond Our Dreams

Ben Watson III

The almost photographic quality of this picture is achieved by retaining full control of each brushstroke and leaving nothing to chance. On the figure the paint is not applied with broad washes, but built up with individual, almost imperceptible brushstrokes. A slightly looser textural approach is used for the background door, leaving the sharpest detail for the dramatically lit face.

Naples yellow body color was spattered onto the door adding a loose spontaneous touch to describe effectively the texture on the weathered door.

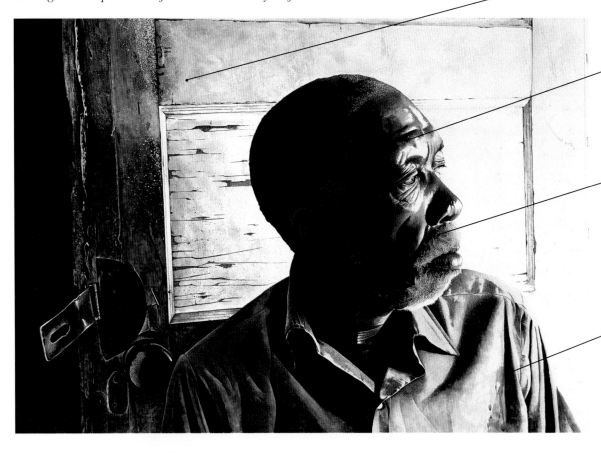

The highlights were created by reserving the white paper to retain pure whites, unsullied by the addition of any paint.

Body color was used to paint the individual gray hairs and those catching the light.

The shirt creases were gradually built up with numerous small applications of semi-transparent paint. A little white body color was used to sharpen the highlights.

River Fiesta

E Gordon West

This painting has an even balance of washes and brushstrokes. The washes are carefully shaped to describe, for example, the bridge and the undulating ripples. The plant and many smaller ripples are composed of precise brushstrokes, that follow specific shapes.

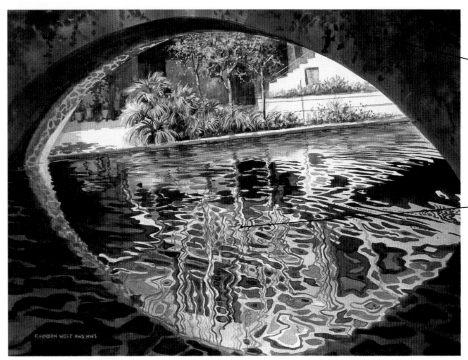

The bridge was painted with a wash applied with a flat brush wet-on-dry. Many brushstrokes remain visible, giving the stonework character.

The center of interest, beautifully framed between the bridge and its reflection, is a composite build-up of wavy lines and carefully controlled abstract patterns.

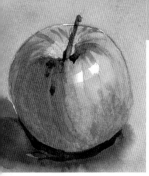

Watercolor is an almost transparent medium, and this is the key to its attractiveness. The translucent quality also dictates the best methods of application. Unlike other mediums when you work in water-color you build up layers from the palest washes to the darkest tones. Careful observation of the subject and planning ensures that the white paper is used for highlights.

Three-stage build-up

There are three overall values in this painting: light, mid-tone, and dark. The palest tones are the yellow on the forehead and the pale gray – almost white – on the snout and nape of the neck. Although these colors are only small areas in the final painting, they make up much of the underpainting. To paint just the light areas light and the dark areas dark would be too fiddly, requiring extremely accurate butting-up and producing too many hard edges.

Building up 1

At the early stages of a painting it can be difficult to imagine how the finished piece will appear. Usually the initial washes represent the background or far distance in which everything appears paler and grayer. Consequently the washes are fainter and you can apply them over a wide area, safe in the knowledge that subsequent layers will be stronger in tone and color and so will cover earlier washes easily. Wait for the surface to be thoroughly dry before adding the next layer, then glide over with a smooth positive stroke.

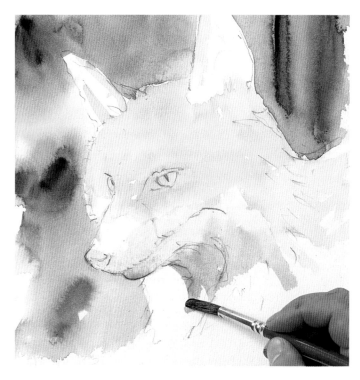

1 Outline the fox's profile by painting the background in a variegated wash of sap green and cadmium yellow, dropping in Payne's gray while wet. When dry, paint the top of the face in dilute Naples yellow, and the bottom in diluted Payne's gray. Leave white paper for highlights.

VARIATION • 1
Skintones

1 *First lay down a wash of raw sienna, loosely suggesting the shape of the face, followed by two consecutive layers of ultramarine as a foundation for the darker areas of the hair and face. Leave areas of white paper showing through.*

2 *Use raw umber to build up the skin tones, and a mixture of ultramarine and cadmium red in the hair and darker features. Apply the paint loosely, allowing some areas to blend and mix, and leaving substantial areas white for the lighter parts of the face.*

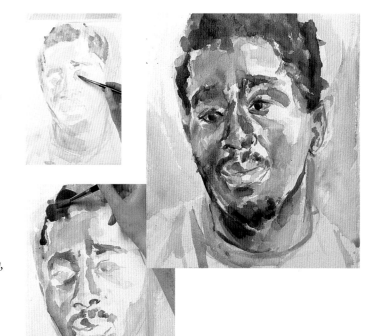

3 *Build up the skin tones and features with burnt sienna and touches of cadmium red. Use a mix of ultramarine and cadmium red for the detail around the eyes. This method of building up and leaving areas unpainted on each wash, forms a rich tapestry of subtle tones.*

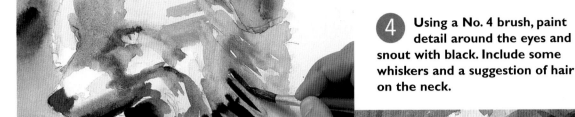

4 Using a No. 4 brush, paint detail around the eyes and snout with black. Include some whiskers and a suggestion of hair on the neck.

5 Enhance the stare in the eyes with some burnt sienna on the eyeball and dots of Chinese white to suggest a sparkle.

2 While still wet, paint dilute burnt umber around the back of the head. Paint the forehead in burnt sienna, allowing it to bleed into the burnt umber. Soften the areas around the eye. Immediately follow with Payne's gray around the eye, nose, and chin. Add streaks of black wet-in-wet, around the neck, back of the head, and into the ears.

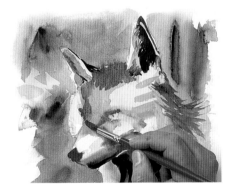

3 Paint a second sap green wash on the background, excluding the yellow area. Before the paint is dry, apply burnt sienna on the forehead, allowing it to bleed into the green between the ears. Continue around the eyes and down the neck.

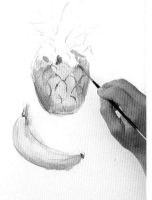

VARIATION • 2
Light to dark

1 *Cover the pineapple with a variegated wash of raw sienna, cadmium orange, and raw umber. Paint the banana with cadmium yellow. Before it dries, brush on raw umber and a mix of yellow and ultramarine.*

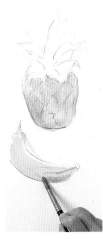

2 *When the pineapple is dry, paint a wash of Venetian red and raw umber onto the sides. Using a rigger, paint detail in the dry, central area and the still damp sides, where the paint will soften slightly. Add some simple detail at either end of the banana.*

3 *Paint the leaf areas in a variegated wash of Prussian blue and raw umber. Go over that with a darker mixture of ultramarine and raw umber to suggest detail. With sepia, paint another wash on either side of the pineapple. Add some dark streaks to the banana.*

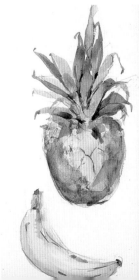

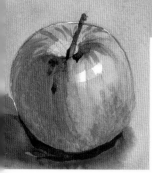

The color of the paper plays an integral part in the overall effect, its whiteness performing a vital backlighting role, illuminating through the color veils. With careful juxtaposition of dark tones, the white paper can appear to glow like sunshine. Each layer of paint absorbs more light, and can carry information in the form of textures. The sum of several layers can confound the eye with depth and detail.

Simple layering

When you are ready to start, begin by careful observation of the subject. Do a visual tone and color breakdown, look for the direction of light and where it falls, and analyze the shadows to see what color they really are. You will need to do a great deal of simplification. Pale washes should go down first; they can be hidden with darker overlays, or made part of a composite build-up.

Building up 2

A careful study and keen observation of the subject before you begin painting can help you to decide on the proper sequence of layers. If you squint your eyes, you will be able to filter out excess detail reducing the subject to simple blocks of tone to be described by each wash. Regardless of distance, lighter patches are separated out from darker patches. It's quite feasible to build up a dark tone with several washes, but it can be difficult to estimate the correct mix in one go because, as the fine pigment soaks into the grain of the paper, the wash will dry paler. Each successive layer should be painted wet-on-dry for maximum intensity.

1 Make a pencil drawing that accurately records the sitter in as few lines as possible. Begin by applying a pale wash of sap green and new gamboge in the window area. Paint burnt sienna on the skin, leaving a thin strip of white to represent reflected light on the face from the window.

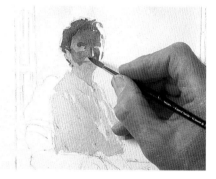

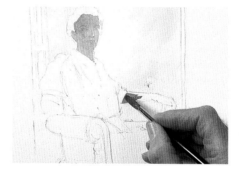

2 Paint a pale cadmium red light wash on the shirt. Use burnt umber for the hair, leaving a little white paper as a highlight. Paint a slightly darker wash of burnt sienna on the face, next to the highlight. Apply a stronger wash of cadmium red light on the chair, with a little ultramarine in the shadow.

VARIATION • I
Building up dark tones

I *This painting has three distinct color stages: pale yellows, bright greens, and darks. Each stage has many overlapping washes. Paint the first washes in this order: lemon yellow, pale ultramarine, yellow ocher, and burnt sienna. These washes will mostly be painted over in the next stages.*

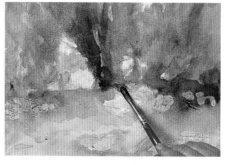

2 *Reserve the brightest highlights with masking fluid, then gradually introduce the green washes, making them pale at first for the more general areas, and progressively building up to darker tones around the tree trunks. Use Hooker's green dark, viridian, and ultramarine with a little Payne's gray.*

3 *Rub off the masking fluid, then with fairly concentrated Payne's gray and burnt sienna paint in the deepest shadows. The finished painting is a comprehensive build-up from light to dark, with the sharpest contrast and point of interest left of center where the sunlight streams from behind the trees.*

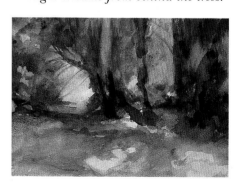

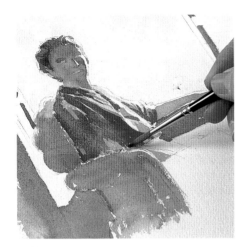

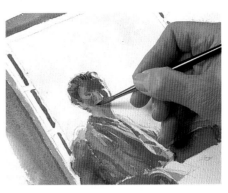

4 Paint another mix of ultramarine and alizarin crimson on the couch, with darker and lighter patches. Mix cadmium red light and burnt sienna for a darker third coat on the face, concentrating on the right, then paint the features with burnt sienna and ultramarine. Loosely paint ultramarine on the pants.

3 Paint a strong mix of burnt umber and ultramarine around the window, leaving white paper for the window frame. Apply a mix of burnt sienna and ultramarine on the left armrest. Mix alizarin crimson and ultramarine and paint on the shirt, leaving the white and some pink areas as areas of lighter tone. Add some patches of burnt umber and ultramarine in the hair.

5 To finish off, add some more sap green to the area outside the window, especially next to the face. Then apply some dark linear detail on the clothing and chair.

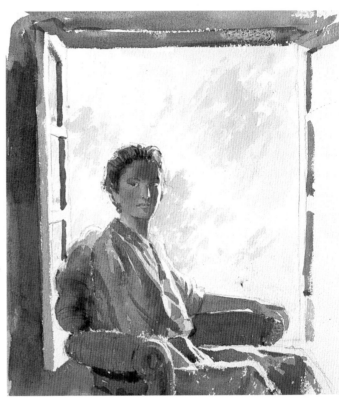

VARIATION • 2
Transparent overlays

1 *The transparent nature of watercolor is perfect for this subject, allowing optical color mixing through overlays. Use cerulean blue for the table and ultramarine for the jug. Start to suggest reflections on the vase with emerald green and ultramarine. Apply a yellow ocher wash for the background.*

2 *Because the multi-faceted crystal vase reflects colors from all around, continue to paint it with a combination of yellow ocher, violet, and cerulean blue in carefully descriptive strokes. Use washes of violet followed by emerald green. Paint the vase and bottle reflections on the table with violet, softening their edges with a clean, damp brush.*

3 *Mix ultramarine and viridian, then paint detail on the bottle. To balance the tones, strengthen the ultramarine on the jug, particularly the part seen through the bottle. Paint an overall emerald green wash on the bottle, leaving a few highlights. Reinforce the violet detail on the vase.*

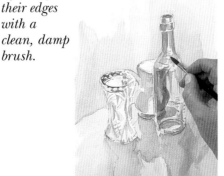

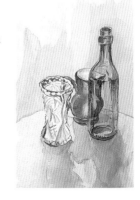

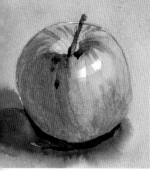

Building up a number of subtle layers gradually to produce deep tone is the sure-footed approach – feeling your way forward as it were – compared with attempting to get the tone right in one go which can increase risk of error. During the build-up, you will also be spending more time analyzing your subject matter, thereby increasing your visual understanding, and producing more pleasing color combinations and an enhanced overall effect.

Building up 3

Diluting pigment with water produces a tint of the pure color. As you overlay different color glazes, the resulting color is altered due to optical mixing; where colors are not physically mixed but laid close together, for example, one on top of the other, they appear to mix. As several faint overlaid washes accumulate and combine, they result in an impressive depth of color. As well as color, you can show detail in each layer, thus producing a complexity difficult to achieve in just one layer.

Optical color mixing

In the first stage, this docklands scene is simplified as a silhouette in one continuous wash. When working this way, it is important to recognize the point at which to stop adding washes – when the correct depth of tone and color is achieved. A few selective highlights can be added later.

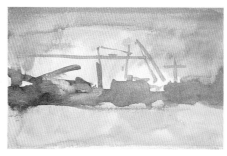

1 Paint the whole area in a graded wash in three separate stages: ultramarine and Payne's gray for the sky, crimson across the middle, and olive green and Davy's gray for the water. When dry, paint a second wash on the sky. Still using the same color, paint the docklands as a simple silhouette.

2 Using cadmium red, paint a horizontal strip at the waterline and add some fine lines for the large crane. Blend ultramarine and Payne's gray in with the red. When dry, glaze some ultramarine, yellow ocher, and burnt sienna detail, and a third wash over the sky.

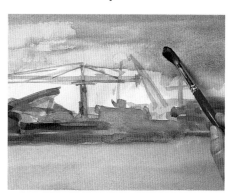

VARIATION • I
Methodical build-up

I *This painting achieves a gradual build-up, creating a sense of depth through increasing tone and color. Begin by painting the sky and distant hills with a faint wash of violet, ivory black, and ultramarine. To create the mottled texture, spray on clean water with an atomizer. Use the same colors for the middle distance.*

2 *When the middle distance is dry, apply a faint wash over it, in the same colors, to soften the strata and get the correct tone. Add Vandyke brown to the same mix and paint the nearer walls.*

3 *Mix lemon yellow and cobalt blue and apply this green in patches.*

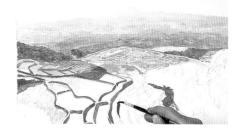

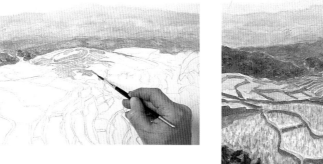

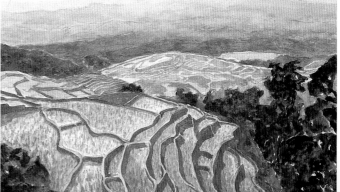

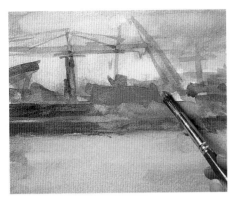

3 Immediately follow with concentrated yellow ocher over the docks, letting it bleed into the still-wet sky. Continue the yellow ocher into the water to represent the warm, hazy reflection of the dock lights.

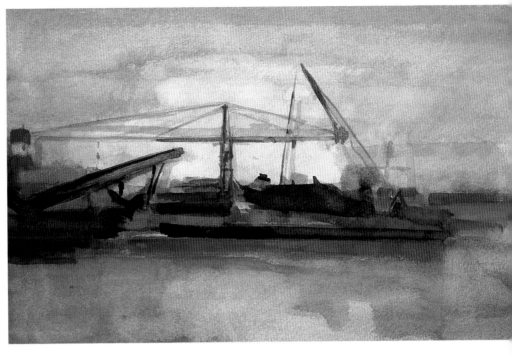

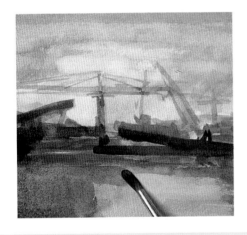

4 When the yellow ocher is only partially dry, blend horizontal strips of concentrated Payne's gray into the docklands foreground. Continue a more diluted Payne's gray over the water, which will still allow the colors beneath to show through. When dry, paint some darker Payne's gray detail over the docks.

5 When dry, paint short strips of cadmium red and yellow ocher between the Payne's gray, including a strip of ocher on the right-hand horizon. Paint concentrated Payne's gray in the central area and add more detail. The gradual build-up of color results in an evocative scene of docklands at dusk.

VARIATION • 2
Variable build-up

1 *In order to utilize the surface texture and create a loose effect, charge a ⅜ inch (1cm) flat brush with ultramarine, and drag it across the top section. Then drop in more paint while the first layer is wet. Apply Winsor green in the same way to the bottom half, adding Prussian blue while wet.*

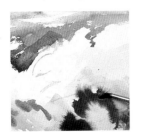

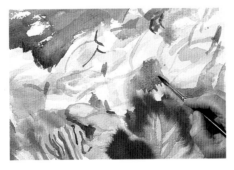

2 *Paint wavy strips of spectrum yellow for the seaweed. When glazed over the blues, this will form fresh greens. Gradually build up the fish and seaweed detail with expressive strokes in mixtures of Prussian blue, spectrum yellow, and burnt sienna, to suggest movement and fluidity.*

3 *Leave white paper to highlight the fish. To emphasize them further, lay another blue wash above them to block out any highlights there. Add a wash of Prussian blue to the seaweed area below and over the lowermost fish, to give the appearance of fish and seaweed mingling.*

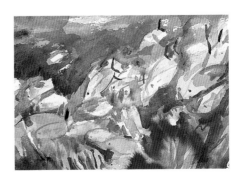

In context

These paintings clearly demonstrate how the transparency of watercolor dictates the technique of building up washes from pale to dark. The full range of tones can be found from broad pale washes to concentrated dark areas of color. In each example the paper remains the sole source of illumination and the contrasting dark tones are a composite build-up of several layers.

Dappled Sunlight, Bridge at Arran

Maurice Read

A light pencil sketch divided this painting into separate areas – for example, trees, bridge, and sky. Each area had its own independent underpainting, a pale version of the final local color. The picture was then built up with a series of small washes, the most complex part being the water ripples, which incorporate colors from the rest of the picture.

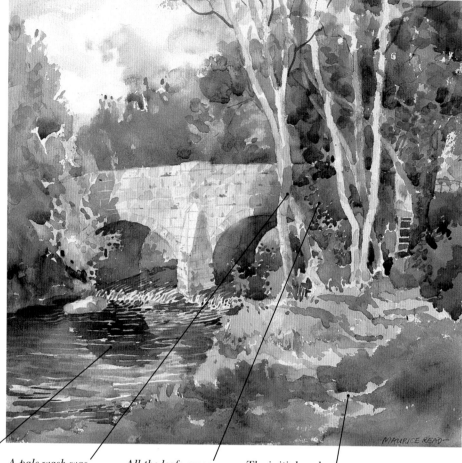

The brown reflection of the bridge and the blue sky are incorporated in the underpainting of the river as a variegated wash. The dark green of the reflections of the trees was laid over the top to suggest ripples.

A pale wash was applied under the trees. The tree trunks were then carefully reserved out of the surrounding green washes so that they stand out from the foliage.

All the leafy areas had a pale green or yellow underpainting that was overlaid with various darker mixtures of green and brown.

The initial underpainting can be seen as a pale Naples yellow, just peeking through the darker wash that overlays it.

Carousel – Brighton Beach

Steve Nicol

Several subtle glazes build up the lively activity in the carousel. The dominant warm yellow underpainting emphasizes the gaiety of the subject, and expressive brushwork adds to the overall energy of the picture.

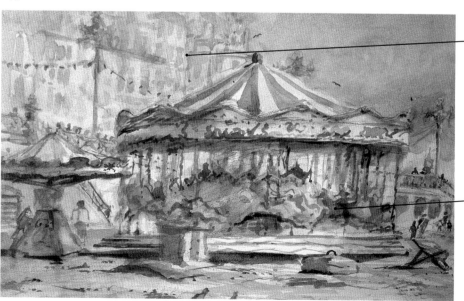

After the first wash of yellow, soft dabs of pink, blue, and brown were applied.

Strokes of diluted pure yellows, reds, and blues were added to bring the whole picture to life. Blue crayon was hatched over the carousel to convey the sense of blurred movement.

Lola on the Bridge

Mark Topham

In this painting the traditional process of building from light to dark was fully exploited. In the sunlit areas the yellow underpainting was left as the final color. The darkest areas, particularly in the foreground, were built up with four glazes of different colors, creating optical mixing of yellow, reds, and blues for depth.

Pale blue body color was used to pick out the few light blue branches over the dark of background.

The overhanging branches are a build-up of four loosely applied washes, with a little scumbling. Each layer allows plenty of underpainting to show through.

The yellow under-painting remains largely uncovered here except for a few odd leaves. It appears fresh and bright and in sharp contrast to the surrounding blues.

Several glazes were applied in the foreground. Masking fluid was applied after each wash to reserve fallen leaves and rocks. Drybrush techniques were used to build up texture.

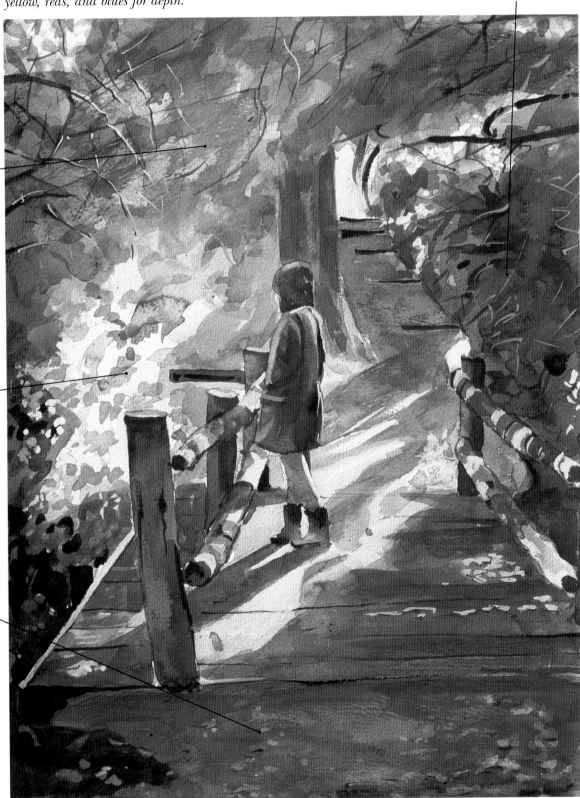

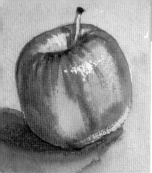

Highlights are the small accents of light that sparkle in a painting, accentuating form and "lifting" the painting off the board. In opaque painting, you would apply them as the finishing touches; in watercolor work, the purest and most luminous highlight is created by leaving areas of the paper unpainted. Consequently, you need to consider the highlights before you start.

Highlights I

The quickest method is to reserve highlights by painting around but not over the points you wish to highlight, as if you were leaving small chinks of light. This method needs careful brushwork and you will need to mark the position of highlights lightly in pencil before you begin painting – with large washes, in particular, it's all too easy to obliterate the highlights. If you want to give your highlights a slightly warm or cool bias (depending on the color of the light source), apply an initial faint wash before reserving. Although faint, it's surprising the difference that this can make. A reserved highlight will have a hard edge unless you paint it onto a damp surface, but you can soften it by redamping and touching gently with a cotton bud.

Reserving hard-edged highlights

Hard-edged highlights are sharp and well suited to this wet nocturnal scene. To achieve them, paint around them onto a dry surface. This way you retain the option of softening them by subsequent wetting. Decide at the outset where the highlights will be and if they will be reserved out of white paper, or yellow or red areas. Then draw them in.

1 Begin with a pencil drawing that clearly shows the position of all light sources and reflections. Use burnt umber and a ⅜ inch (1cm) flat brush to paint a wash all over the painting, omitting highlights or parts that will be bright yellow. This clearly establishes areas of light and dark.

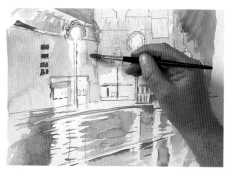

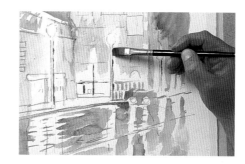

2 Paint further washes of cadmium red and cadmium yellow deep. Extend the yellow into all of the lit-up central area, leaving only the white highlights. Paint thin, dry strokes of red and yellow around the street lamps. Use red for the bricks along the corner of the building on the right.

VARIATION • I
Reserving soft highlights

1 *Paint an initial graded wash of yellow ocher. Turn the board so that the concentrated color is at the bottom of the picture. While the paint is still wet, paint in strokes of fairly strong Antwerp blue, leaving areas of pale ocher for the clouds.*

2 *While the paint is still wet and working fast, apply fairly strong Payne's gray in the pale ocher areas. Leave enough room around the gray for it to spread and still leave some areas unpainted for highlights.*

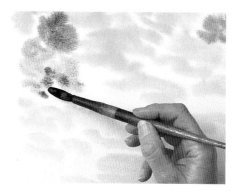

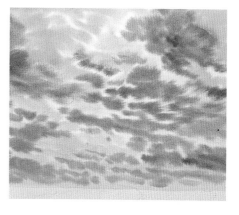

3 *Tilt the board slightly to give the clouds a little direction. This random, unpredictable technique produces a soft, pleasing effect that is easy to achieve. The whole of the process is done wet-in-wet.*

5 Using the same brush and the same technique, paint ultramarine around the automobile headlamps. Fill in the automobile body, too. Add dark touches with ultramarine and burnt umber where needed around the painting, particularly the edge of the sidewalk. Paint one final wash of burnt umber with a little ultramarine to subdue parts of the buildings, further highlighting the lamps and reflections.

3 Paint ultramarine into the darker outlying areas and between the bright reflections on the road. This contrasting cool color will "light up" the highlights.

4 Using a finer brush, build up further yellow and red strokes around the streetlights. Work small touches of concentrated yellow around the lit-up area, particularly the street surface, to reflect the light source above.

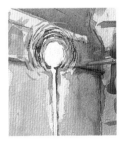

VARIATION • 2
Creating soft-edged highlights

1 *Draw the jug, vase, and flowers, indicating the highlights. Paint the jug in Winsor emerald, lemon yellow, and chrome yellow, working around the reserved highlights, which will initially be hard-edged. Gently rub the highlights with a fine natural sponge, softening the edges and lifting off excess paint.*

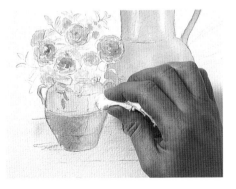

2 *Lay a second wash of Winsor emerald on the jug and repeat the process. When you come to do the highlight for the vase, you can soften the highlight with a piece of rolled kitchen paper. This is more absorbent, so be careful not to lift off more paint than intended.*

3 *Complete the painting by adding the detail of the flowers and foliage, and a suggestion of background.*

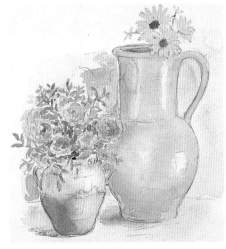

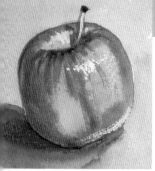

If you accidentally paint over those tiny highlights, all is not lost. Dry paint can be removed, and this may be the best solution so as not to interrupt the flow of brushwork. Depending on your choice of method, you can either produce sharp, speckled highlights or soft-edged ones.

Highlights 2

To get back to the original white ground, you can scratch, scrape, rub, or scrub the paper. Scratch out a fine line with a scalpel point; as you catch the high points on the paper surface you will create a speckled line. For a soft highlight, rub a hard eraser on a dry surface, or scrub with a damp bristle brush and dab with a tissue. If you use a thin template with this technique, you will produce a hard edge. For gentle highlights a cotton bud, sponge, or sable brush can be rubbed onto a dry or damp surface to lift off paint. All these techniques need sensitive application so as not to cause too much friction. (For further explanation, see **Lifting Out**, page 94.)

Using a hard eraser

Using a hard eraser is a good way of creating soft highlights. The process is very gradual and requires repeated strokes to produce results. The darker the ground color, the greater the contrast you can achieve. To keep straight edges or confined areas, use a template as described in Lifting Out *on page 94.*

1 With a large squirrel mop brush, paint washes of cobalt blue, ultramarine, and olive green, omitting the duck. Paint a second wash of ultramarine over the right and foreground areas to darken them. Leave to dry.

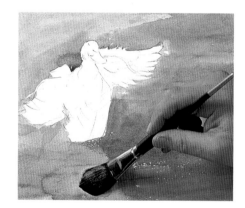

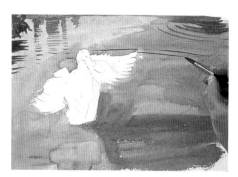

2 With the underpainting done, mix olive green and cobalt blue and paint the reflections of the bank and the ripples on the water.

VARIATION • I
Scratching out highlights

1 *Begin by applying a gradated wash in light red over the whole picture area. While still wet, drop Payne's gray and Antwerp blue in the upper and lower thirds of the picture, avoiding the horizon area. Leave to dry, then paint the land with Payne's gray.*

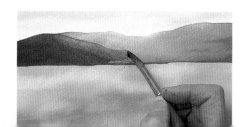

2 *Apply another, darker wash on the distant water. Leave to dry. Then, using a razor blade, gently scratch out long horizontal lines, allowing the blade to skip over the rough paper surface to form white beads.*

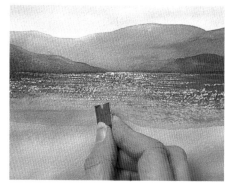

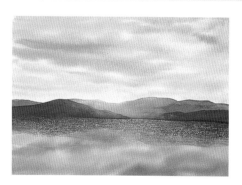

3 *The soft, blended background and dark horizon contrast with and enhance the calm, sparkling water, producing an ethereal effect. Because of the speed of watercolor work, you should be able to complete this evocative painting in under an hour.*

3 With ultramarine, build up a further layer of blue in broad, curved strokes to show the movement on the water surface. These support and amplify the smaller green ripples, giving the water its shape and suggesting the duck's movements.

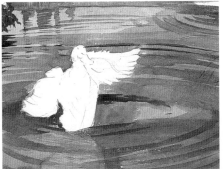

5 Make sure that the paint is thoroughly dry, then with a hard eraser rub repeatedly but not too hard in long curved strokes to remove some of the blue between the darker strips. These soft highlights represent the crests of the gentle ripples.

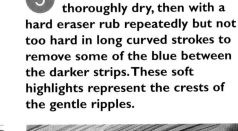

6 The finished water surface is an accumulation of many different effects, including broad washes, hard lines, dry-brush, and soft, erased highlights. These effects all work in unison, with none dominating the others.

4 Paint the reeds on the right in burnt umber and Payne's gray, knifing out the color a little on top. Paint the shadows on the duck in ultramarine and olive green, and use yellow ocher and burnt sienna for the beak. Paint the darker ripples in indigo.

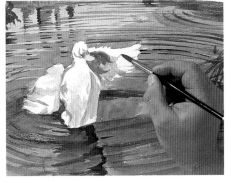

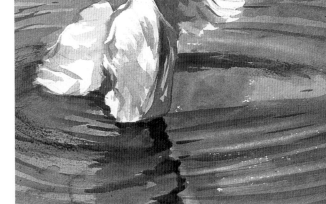

VARIATION • 2
Using a bristle brush and tissue

1 *Apply a background wash of cadmium yellow and magenta. Paint the folds of the cloth and the floor in ultramarine. Overpaint the cloth with cadmium red and magenta. Overlay a wash of emerald green on the floor.*

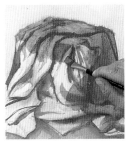

2 *When the paint is dry, scrub the highlight areas with a bristle brush to soften the pigment. Use a No. 1 or 2 bristle brush with short hairs: this gives more precise control. Then dab off the softened pigment with a tissue.*

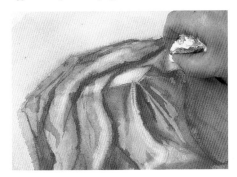

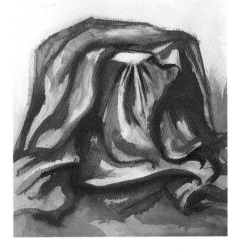

3 *Paint a final wash of magenta around the highlights to crisp up the edges and deepen the shaded areas.*

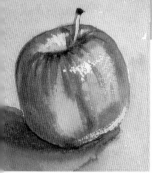

Highlights 3

If there are too many fiddly highlights in an area that you want to treat with broad, flowing brushstrokes, masking fluid is the answer. It can free you to paint unhindered. Alternatively, using body color allows you to put highlights in at the end, when it's easier to judge where and how bright they should be.

With masking fluid (see Masking, page 92) you can paint highlights in fine detail and with infinite variety, the only drawback being that they may appear mechanical, with hard edges. You can solve this problem by wetting and stroking over the highlights afterward with a bristle brush. To reserve tinted highlights, paint over a dry wash with masking fluid. Once painted on, allow it to dry before resuming painting and let the painting dry before rubbing the fluid off. Using body color (see page 122) will allow you greater freedom to paint highlights in with a variety of brushstrokes. Dry-brushed highlights (see page 63) are also effective: mix Chinese white into a thick paste and add a hint of yellow to make it glow.

Body color

Body color is the most effective way of creating tiny highlights. With masking fluid the results are not known until you rub it off, but body color is more controllable and gives immediate results.

1 **With the pencil drawing completed, paint yellow gamboge over the orange, the peel, and segments. Paint the shadow under the serviette with ultramarine and violet.**

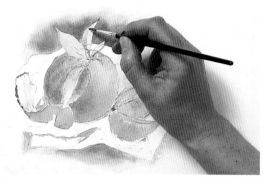

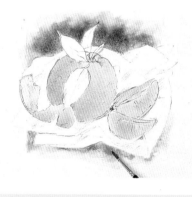

2 **While the orange is still damp, paint in the shaded areas with cadmium red deep mixed with the yellow. Mix chrome yellow with Prussian blue and paint the leaves. Add a second wash to the leaves when the first is dry.**

VARIATION • 1
Reserving highlights with masking fluid

1 *Apply an ultramarine wash to the wall behind the fountain. Lay a pale wash of cadmium red over the areas to have highlights. Allow to dry thoroughly and paint on the masking fluid with a No. 2 brush, and leave to dry. (You can speed up the drying by using a hairdryer.)*

2 *Continue painting with sap green and indigo for the trees and grass, violet and ultramarine for the wall, burnt sienna, burnt umber and violet for the fountain. When thoroughly dry, rub off the masking fluid to expose the pale pink highlights.*

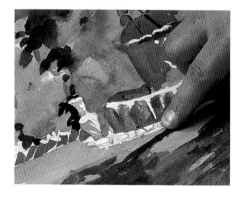

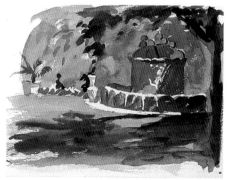

3 *Almost all of this picture is done with a large brush in broad washes, a free technique only possible if the highlights are reserved in advance.*

3 With a stronger mix of mostly cadmium red deep and a little yellow gamboge, build up the texture of the orange peel with a series of small washes and small flecks of paint, made with a No. 0 brush. Use the same color mix on the segments. Apply Payne's gray for the shadows under and around the orange.

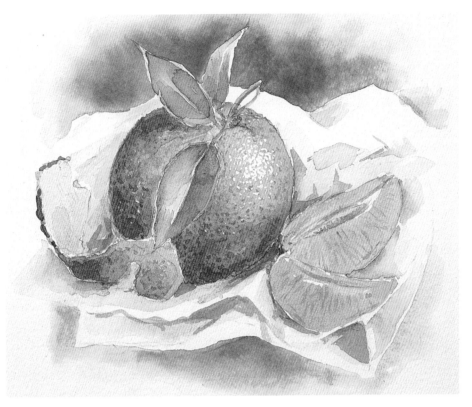

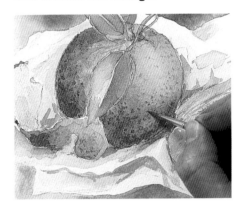

4 Use concentrated Chinese white and a No. 0 brush to paint dotted highlights on the peel. Apply a greater concentration of dots in the center of the highlight area, then thin them using smaller touches as you move outward.

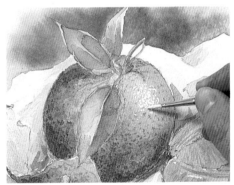

5 The method of applying the dots helps to describe the spherical shape. The specks of white paint are almost entirely confined to one area, which produces a greater impact.

VARIATION • 2
Broader highlights

1 *You will need the freedom to paint loosely behind the complicated shapes of the chairs and plant highlights, while retaining freshness of the paper. Begin by completely covering the chairs and the highlighted leaves with masking fluid. Then paint the background and shadows in browns, blues, and muted violet.*

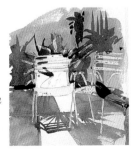

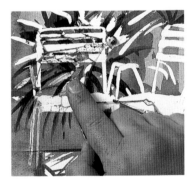

2 *When the paint is dry, rub off the masking fluid and continue painting onto the now exposed white paper.*

3 *Paint sap green onto some of the exposed leaves. Paint pale strips of cerulean blue and cadmium red to give the chairs a little shape.*

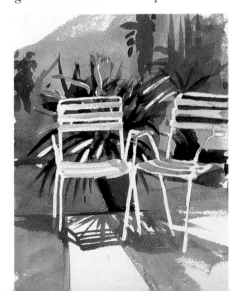

In context

Each stage in a painting plays an important part in determining the finished result, although some stages are not immediately obvious. Highlights, however, do not fall into this category. They send a clear message and are intended to catch the eye. These paintings provide examples of different types of highlights produced in a number of ways.

Cascade

Beverly Hallam

This subject provides dramatic contrasts between dark shadows and bright highlights. The hard-edged highlights were obtained by the use of masking fluid painted over a broad area on the table and used in several stages for the flowers. Even though the highlights are very sharp, they are balanced by plenty of softness elsewhere in the picture. Hayle Mill Linen 21 paper was used, which explains the interesting soft, grainy texture.

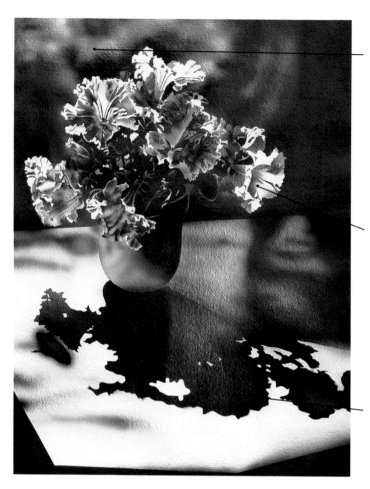

Soft background highlights were formed by painting wet-in-wet and lifting off with tissue. They suggest the light source but are designed to avoid conflict with the main subject.

The hard-edged highlights were the result of strong backlighting, imparting a strong sense of drama.

An almost pure black is butted against an equally pure white. The contrast couldn't be greater, and the result is stunning.

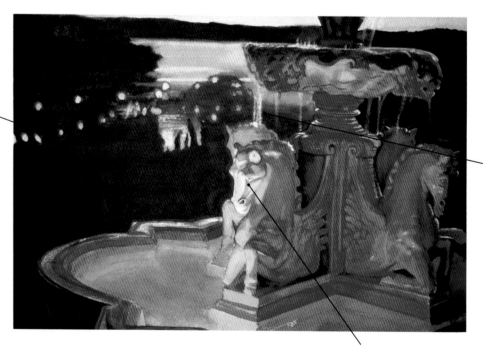

These highlights have been softened with red painted on the inside edge with a fine brush. They represent light sources and this treatment gives the impression of twinkling.

This backlit highlight formed by the water cascading from the fountain was scraped back out of the dry paint. This technique is also evident in other parts of the painting.

Night Vision IV – Tablerock Lake

Henry Dixon

The highlights in this painting are soft, each one surrounded by its own little red halo. These highlights were reserved out of the warm underpainting by painting around them.

The soft yellow highlights on the fountain were carefully blended and modeled to help describe the forms.

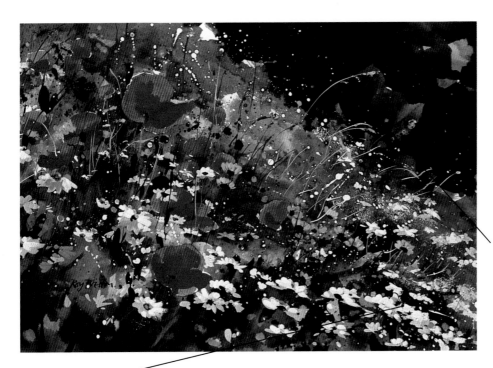

Poppies and Daisies
Roy Preston

Body color is a good way of producing highlights and can be used in conjunction with other methods. Highlights rendered in this way may not appear very bright, while the paint is drying, as the paint absorbs a little of the color underneath. But this technique provided great freedom and extra ability to control the application.

Body color is spattered on with flicks of the paintbrush adding a spontaneous spattering of sparkling dots.

The white daisy petals have been painted with small dabs of thick white body color. Some petals are slightly muted with touches of blue.

John G. Munson
Greg Tisdale

This painting demonstrates the techniques of reserving highlights with masking fluid. The masking fluid was both spattered on in a fine spray and dabbed on with the tip of a brush. The hard-edged character of these highlights is important in conveying the necessary sparkle of the glistening crests of the wave.

The froth in the ship's wake was created by a combination of finely sprayed masking fluid and painted dots which reserved the paper surface for the highlights.

Elongated brushstrokes of masking fluid were painted over a pale-tinted watercolor surface of the same color as the sky to produce slightly muted highlights. These are reflections of the boat's sail, as opposed to the brighter reflections of sunlight.

Dispersed white dots are the result of masking the white paper. The pale ripples that reflect the sky, were produced by masking over the yellow underpainting that also forms the lower part of the sky.

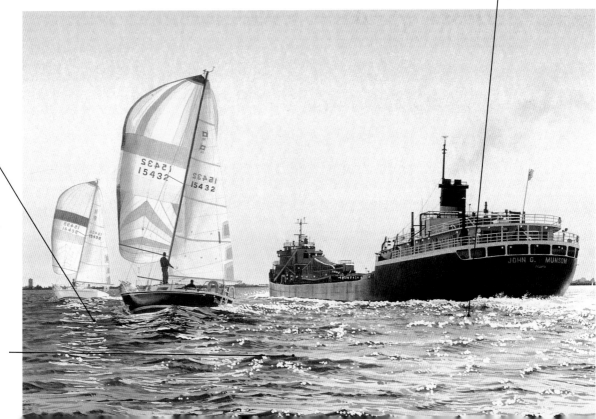

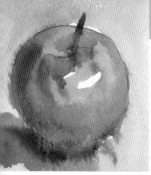

Wet-in-wet I

This is one of the most exciting watercolor techniques. As you add paint to a wet or damp surface, the paint flows, taking on a life of its own in an unpredictable way. This way of working is probably the cause of the majority of "happy accidents." The final effect can be magical and seductive.

Wet the surface with clean water and paint directly onto it while it is still damp. Alternatively, apply paint to a dry surface and add more paint while it is still wet. The speed at which subsequent work takes place is largely determined by the drying time of the paint, so do not wet more than you need or the drying time will extend unnecessarily. Once the paint is released onto the surface, you can tilt the board to direct the flow of water. Keep some tissue paper handy to mop up excess water and use a hairdryer to halt the blending at the desired point.

Wet-in-wet magic

With such an unpredictably fluid technique, only a simple preliminary sketch is necessary. Use light pencil marks because you don't want them to show in the final picture, and a heavy pencil line will run and dirty the fresh colors that are needed for this subject.

1 Flood the whole picture area with clean water and let it soak in for a few seconds. With a large, flexible brush such as a squirrel-hair, paint in ultramarine, Payne's gray, and violet in separate areas defined by your sketch.

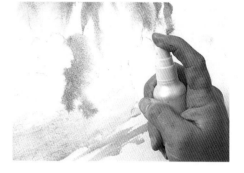

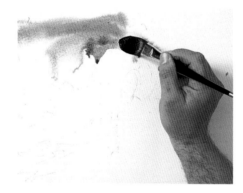

2 Prolonged wet-in-wet painting is required for this picture. If the paint starts to dry halfway through, creating unwanted hard edges, spray on clean water with an atomizer. This will take effect in seconds, softening hard edges and enhancing the flow. Allow this first wash to dry.

VARIATION · I
Wet-in-wet wash

1 *No drawing is necessary for this freehand painting. Mix a sufficient quantity of Antwerp blue to cover the whole picture and apply a graded wash, with a greater concentration of color on the top and gradually becoming more dilute toward the bottom. Do this with the board leaning at a 30° angle toward you.*

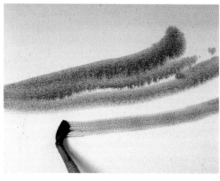

2 *Before the paint has time to soak in, load the brush with a stronger mix of Payne's gray and Antwerp blue. With sideways sweeping motions, paint the mix into the wet surface. This will spread out and merge in all directions, running downward slightly due to the slope of the board.*

3 *When completely dry, paint the horizon line in Payne's gray. Notice how the clouds have faded a little during drying.*

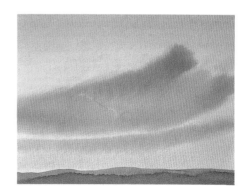

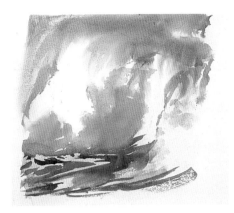

3 Subsequent washes need more definition, so pre-wet only selected areas. Apply cerulean blue in the central area, softening some parts with water. Paint ultramarine streaks at the bottom, then stroke over them with a wet brush. Allow the two areas to fuse.

5 Go around the picture, adding a few dark blue spots and very pale, undulating washes in the foam. Finally, dab spots of Chinese white as foam in any places you have accidentally painted over. Then add streaks of dry-brush white over the blue for texture.

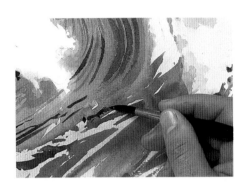

4 Mix a little emerald green with cerulean blue and a hint of Payne's gray, and use to give the wave more shape underneath. Then, with a darker mix, paint the curve lines underneath. Add a touch of black to the same mix and paint in the small, dark areas immediately under the crest.

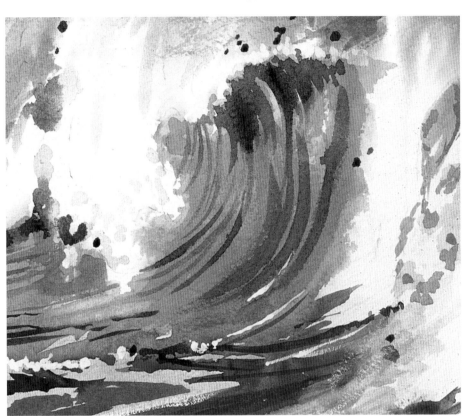

VARIATION • 2
Tilting the board

1 *The wet-in-wet technique is ideally suited to skies. First wet the picture area and drop in new gamboge, rose madder, and Antwerp blue in horizontal strokes. Use the most concentrated blue at the top. Tilt the board slightly toward you so that the colors run downward.*

2 *Working horizontally and from the top down, randomly drop in Payne's gray in fluid, concentrated drops. Let this run down and through the previous wash creating interesting patterns. Vary the effect by tilting the board down to the right.*

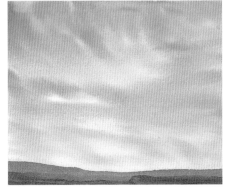

3 *Some of the original colors should show between the clouds. If not, lift off some wet Payne's gray with a "thirsty" brush and apply some more original color. When dry, paint the land with Payne's gray, then new gamboge.*

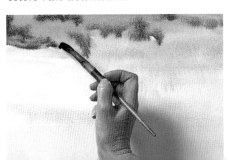

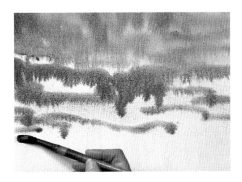

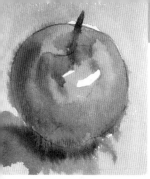

As you let the water do some of the work for you, you relinquish a degree of control.

A wet-in-wet wash makes an ideal background for working over, and perfectly describes many natural phenomena. When painting layers of atmosphere in a landscape, you need to give vague definition to distant objects. You can also use this technique to blur less important parts of a composition so that they have less prominence.

Wet-in-wet 2

As you drop paint into a wet surface, the wetness acts as a vehicle for movement, diffusing and bleeding the colors – working on a dry surface, on the other hand, is like applying the brakes. You can work paint into a large wash using a big brush in a long sweep to release a strip of color that will bleed sideways. Alternatively, you can drop small amounts of paint into small washes to produce random, flowering effects. After a wash has dried, it can be dampened again with a brush or an atomizer (which will dampen the surface without disturbing previous layers), and then apply another layer. Thicker paint with a less wet surface will reduce the amount of bleeding.

Painting into a wet surface

During pre-wetting of the surface a large brush or sponge is used, and a lot of water will soak into the surface. If you apply the paint when the surface is too wet, much of it will soak away into the paper. Wait for a few seconds before applying paint, or mop up any excess water with a tissue.

1 Keep most pencil work above the waterline so you can treat the water freely. Pre-wet the water area with clean water and apply olive green, Indian yellow, burnt sienna, and violet down and across the water in wavy brushstrokes, letting them bleed into the damp surface.

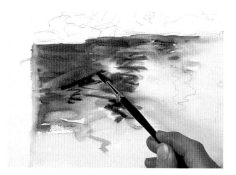

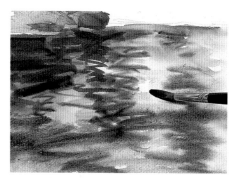

2 Continue this process until the whole water area is filled in. The brushstrokes of this initial wash will dissipate losing their definition. As the surface dries a little, brush concentrated strokes of Vandyke brown and olive green over the water to represent ripples. These will fur.

VARIATION • 1
Colors fusing together

1 With a 2B pencil, define three main areas: ground, smoke, and trees, adding a little detail. Brush a pale wash of cobalt blue and burnt umber over the tree area. Before this is dry, loosely paint patches of ultramarine into the smoke area, allowing it to blend with the tree area.

2 Brush a pale strip of sap green and burnt sienna on the ground and allow them to fuse together. When dry, mix cerulean blue and new gamboge. Paint this on the leaves and burnt umber on the trunks, allowing them to blend together leaving no hard edge between trunks and leaves.

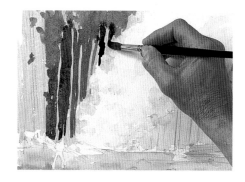

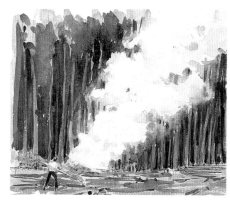

3 Blend the trunks and smoke on the bottom right in the same way. When all the wet-in-wet blending is completed, finish off by painting the foreground detail and figures with a fine pointed No. 4 brush.

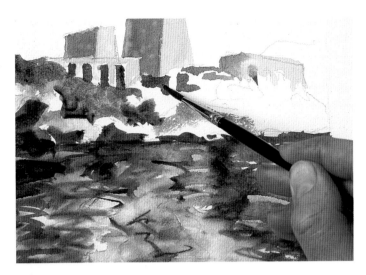

5 Paint the sky with cerulean blue outlining the temple. The temple gives the picture definition and perspective but is deliberately understated. In contrast, the water effect conveys excitement and energy.

3 Using Naples yellow, Vandyke brown, and olive green, paint the temple and trees on a dry surface but apply the trees loosely. This will result in a crisper image, to contrast with the water.

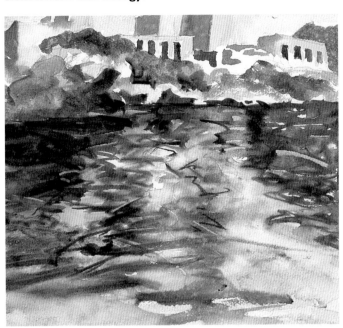

4 In this close-up of the water, you can see the build-up of paint in the various stages of drying. There is a lot of motion in the water so the reflections still retain the original colors of the riverbank but not its shape.

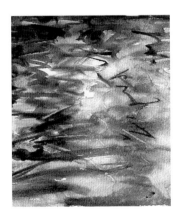

VARIATION • 2
Wet-in-wet in restricted areas

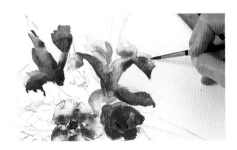

3 *Paint leaves and flowers with a succession of small washes, working back into each one. Keep the detail to a minimum so as not to lose the soft effect.*

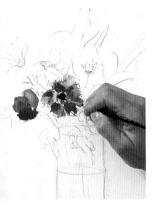

1 *The technique here is to paint the initial flower wash onto a dry surface, then work more paint into the wet area. Use Winsor violet, permanent rose, and Payne's gray on the first two flowers.*

2 *Paint the iris in Winsor violet and cadmium yellow pale, all the time working further into the wet areas with clean water droplets or concentrated paint. To add extra interest, lift out small areas with a sponge. As each flower dries, you can repeat the process, adding two or three layers to each flower.*

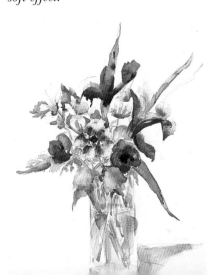

In context

With the absence of brushmarks and the presence of free-flowing pigment and water, the use of wet-in-wet techniques in all of these paintings is unmistakable. Each work demonstrates different ways of manipulating the spontaneous characteristics of watercolor paint applied in this way.

Reflections of June

James Harvey Taylor

This is an example of a watercolorist in his element. Almost the entire painting is made up of wet-in-wet paintwork. Hard edges have been formed where necessary by painting next to a dry surface. Detail is kept to a minimum, giving the atmospheric qualities of the scene full rein.

The sky was painted first by dampening the paper then dropping in different blues and pink. The break in the clouds was produced by lifting off with tissue.

This dramatic diagonal land edge was produced by wetting the river area, leaving the left bank dry then dropping in dark paint to represent the reflections of the trees. The dark paint bled into the water, leaving a hard edge on the left bank where the paper had remained dry.

This small clump of trees was loosely brushed onto the dry surface, followed by additional darker paint added around the base. The paler trunks were knifed out before the paint dried.

The right bank was painted when the river was dry. Long strokes of dark paint were pulled over the dry edge to produce the effect of dark blades of grass.

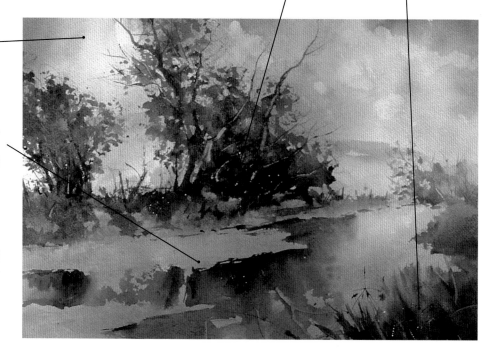

Hunstanton Beach

Alan Oliver

This painting has been treated with broad gentle washes. Colors of similar tone have been added to the sky to produce soft cloud formations. The objects along the promenade were suggested with dabs of wet-in-wet, then clarified in ink. Body color was used for the figures.

The brown of the tower was painted wet-in-wet. It subtly bleeds into the sky, creating a pleasant soft-focus effect that suggests the hazy weather of the scene.

The beach was painted in a broad wash, with streaks of brown added into the wet paint. These spread and softened, creating the impression of wet sand and tide marks. While the paint was still damp, a fine spray of water was applied with an atomizer, creating a mottled texture.

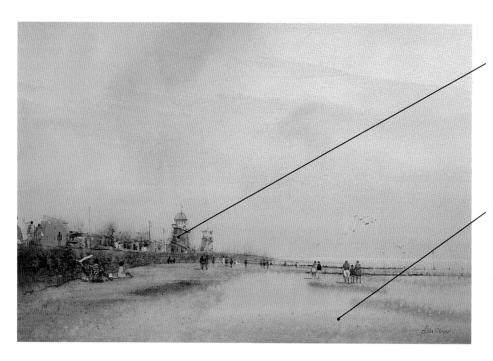

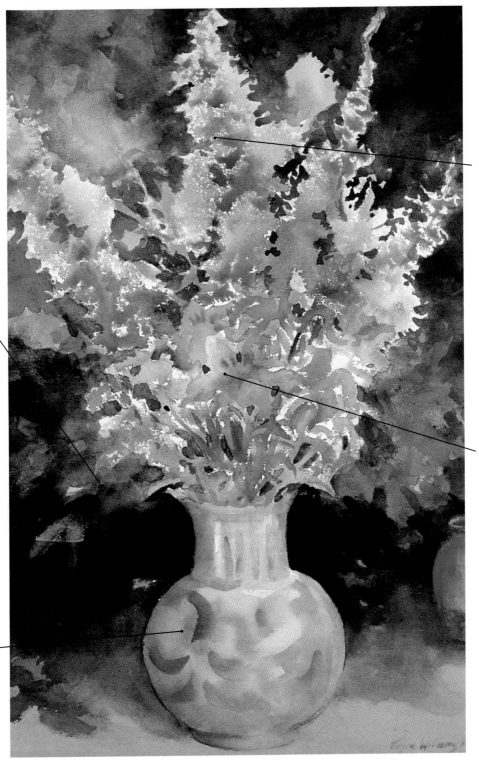

The blue and lilac flowers were painted before the background by painting small areas, dabbing with tissue to break up the paint, and dropping further blues into the wet areas. Various exciting textures are the result.

The vase and flowers are largely defined by outlining with the dark background wash. This was achieved by repeatedly adding browns and blacks to the gradually drying surface to build up the required dark tone.

The orange flowers were painted wet-on-dry, which gives definition to the long petals. These flowers contain very little bleeding of paint, although small amounts of a darker color were dropped into the wet orange.

The vase is treated simply by working both wet-in-wet and wet-on-dry to achieve varying degrees of clarity. The blending of the curved blue brushstrokes is suggestive of the decoration on its rounded form.

Lilies and Delphiniums

Joyce Williams

This vivacious still life was painted by confining the wet-in-wet areas within restricted boundaries. The painting was built up with many wet-in-wet brush strokes, rather than with broad washes. A lot of exciting blending is apparent, particularly in the flowers.

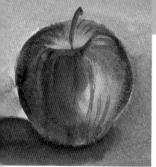

Hard and soft edges

The transition from hard to soft edges is a classic feature of water-color painting. By dissolving parts of an outline, you help an object to harmonize better with its surroundings, producing a stronger interrelationship. In general this occurs spontaneously but with a little control you can guide the effect, and there are several ways to do this.

If you want to create both hard and soft edges (otherwise known as "lost and found"), then, before painting, wet only the areas corresponding to the soft edges. As you fill in the defined area and come up against the wet surface, the edge of the painted area will soften. If you have already painted wet-on-dry (see page 46), simply add clean water with a soft brush to the required edge and softly blend the water into the paint. Another good method is to spray with an atomizer, and after a few seconds the edges will soften. Alternatively, if you want to soften an edge after it is dry, dampen only the required area and soften with a bristle brush or cotton bud.

Produced wet-on-dry

This painting has predominantly hard edges, but the few soft edges help to loosen up the images, allowing the eye to travel around the composition more easily. It is painted mainly wet-on-dry and therefore the softening is done with the brush immediately after the application of the paint. The middle statue has hard edges on the left, but a soft edge where the head should be and behind the legs, which also merge into the oval headpiece beneath.

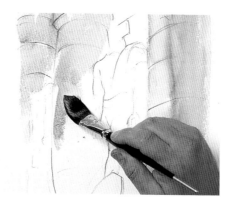

1 **After completing your preliminary drawing, paint washes of yellow ocher, burnt sienna, and violet, freely over the pillars, without too much concern for the edges and boundaries. Keep violet mainly to the left side and burnt sienna to the right.**

2 **Drop further paint into these washes so that the colors mingle and flow, loosely suggesting the shapes. Paint the center statue with violet and burnt sienna. The pencil marks indicate the edges of the shapes, but do not keep the paint rigidly within these boundaries.**

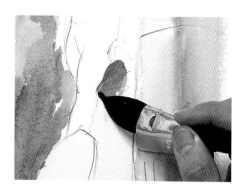

VARIATION • I
Produced wet-in-wet

1 *No detailed preliminary drawing is needed. Paint a pale wash of alizarin crimson for the sky. When that is dry, use ultramarine for the back-ground trees and immediately paint loose washes of Hooker's green for the foreground. Allow these last three washes to merge wet-in-wet.*

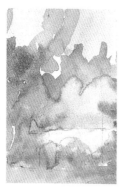

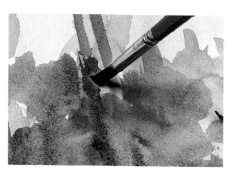

2 *Paint a loose wash of olive green, Hooker's green, and Prussian blue across the middle section, to represent trees and foliage. While that is wet, apply Payne's gray in vertical brush-strokes for the tree trunks. This will form hard edges above and below the central wash, but leave soft edges in the central wet area.*

3 *The tree trunks are painted with alternate hard and soft edges as they rise through the dappled shadows and leaves. The shapes appear to float and shimmer, making this painting an atmospheric play of light.*

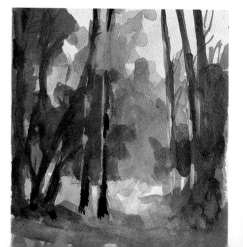

3 Continue to work on the center statue. Paint the legs, the shadows underneath, and the crown below. Smooth out any hard edges that form by running a damp brush over them, to encourage the merging of the areas of different colors.

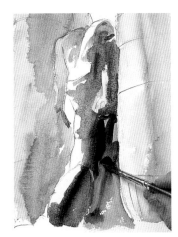

5 Add further washes of violet and burnt sienna to the other two pillars. Apply black between the central pillar and central statue, leaving a hard edge where it meets the statue and soft edge on the pillar. When the washes are dry, paint the detail and hieroglyphics on the pillars.

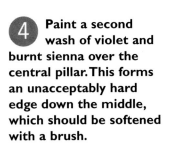

4 Paint a second wash of violet and burnt sienna over the central pillar. This forms an unacceptably hard edge down the middle, which should be softened with a brush.

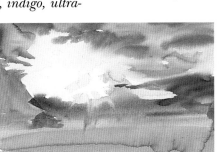

6 Within the framework of horizontal shapes the paint was applied freely and loosely with a limited palette to maintain unity. The fine detail of the hieroglyphics help to define the shapes and pull the composition together. If there had been only crisp, sharp edges throughout, the painting would appear much stiffer and less expressive.

VARIATION • 2
Combining wet and dry

1 *Apply a broad wash of Naples yellow across the sky. Paint into this wet-in-wet with burnt sienna, indigo, ultramarine, and, at the horizon, Prussian blue. Paint a flat wash of Prussian blue for the sea. The edges at this stage are almost all soft.*

2 *When dry, re-wet some of the surface and add more concentrated indigo in selected areas for the clouds. Where the paint touches dry parts of the surface, hard edges are formed and where it touches wet areas, the edges are soft. When the sky is dry, paint the mountain and waves wet-on-dry. Add small amounts of water at the base of some of the waves to soften the edges. Leave hard edges for the crests of the waves.*

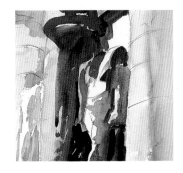

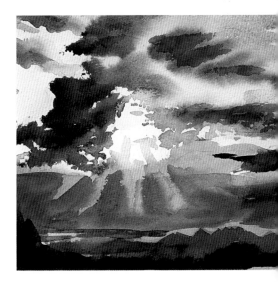

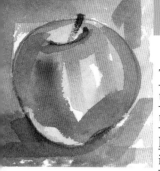

The brush remains the most versatile tool for applying paint. A bewildering array of brushes produces different marks, for different applications. It's advisable to have a wide selection of brushes, and inevitably you will discover which ones suit your style of painting. The handling of the brush is where the real skill lies, and this comes with practice.

Brushmarks

The way in which you hold your brush is an extension of your posture. If you come in close, resting the heel of your hand on the board, you will hold the brush like a pen for detail and fine control. As you move back to gain better perspective, you will hold it with a looser grip and at the end of the handle, which allows freer brushwork. A short-haired brush is firmer and allows greater control, while a long-haired brush is more flexible and is suited to looser brushwork. The rigger is a fine, long-haired brush that makes drawing long lines (straight or curved) easier. For painting detail, a mahl stick can be helpful in steadying your hand.

Self-styled brushes

As your skills develop, you will be able to turn a 1 inch (2.5cm) decorator's brush into a craftsman's tool. Exploit the stiffer hair to produce a variety of textures. Always look for new ways in which to make marks. Generally, you begin with a large brush, progress to a medium brush, and finish with a fine, pointed brush.

1 For your drawing, you need only do a series of small marks. As they will show in the finished picture, a hard line drawing is not required. With a 1 inch (2.5cm) hake, paint mixes of cadmium red and yellow with violet for the village with simple, horizontal and vertical brushmarks.

2 For the trees, make a different set of marks with a ⅜ inch (1cm) decorator's brush, flicking the strokes at different angles. Use ultramarine, indigo, cadmium yellow, and burnt sienna.

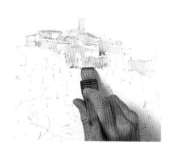

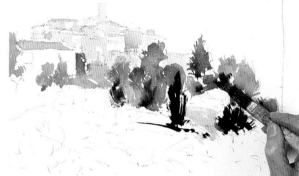

VARIATION • I
Calligraphic brushmarks

1 *With a ⅜ inch (1cm) flat brush, mix ultramarine and violet, then paint the first layer with a mixture of brushmarks. Work with a flexible wrist movement to attain graceful swirls and twists, and keep the arm away from the surface for maximum freedom of movement.*

2 *Paint washes of burnt umber and Hooker's green for the banks, taking the colors over the previous paint. Using burnt umber and a No. 3 brush, add in detail on the rocks.*

3 *The elegant brushwork and highly transparent washes impart a freshness evocative of the subject. The water appears fluid and alive, and there is a perfect balance between washes and brushstrokes.*

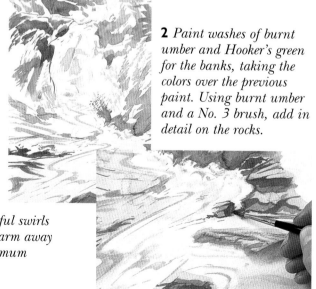

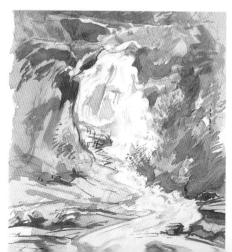

3 Build up the vegetation, switching brushes to create variety. Exploit the paper tooth and leave white paper to highlight the brushmarks. This will help to retain a light, airy feeling reminiscent of a Mediterranean village bathed in sunlight. With a fine brush, add detail such as trunks and branches.

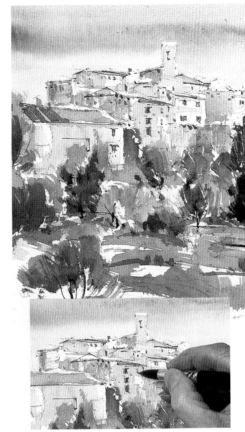

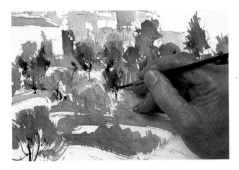

4 Continue building up the picture, with a careful balance of techniques and tones. In this painting, there is no underpainting or build-up of washes, but rather an assortment of small brushmarks which results in a little wet-in-wet blending of colors when one mark overlaps another.

5 Use burnt sienna applied with the point of a round brush to hint at the shapes and shadows of the roofs and windows.

6 The large expanse of white paper in the immediate foreground leads the viewer into the picture. This transition from bare paper to painted surface draws the eye into the construction of the picture.

VARIATION • 2
Brushmarks build-up

1 *Apply a graded wash of pale burnt sienna at the top, yellow ocher in the middle, and magenta at the bottom. Suggest the docks with dilute Payne's gray. Paint the ripples and the boat's reflection in Hooker's green and burnt umber. Start to build up the boat with Indian red and black.*

2 *Paint a second wash of Indian red mixed with a little black on the boat. Mix black with Hooker's green and paint the dark ripples with horizontal brushmarks and squiggly lines.*

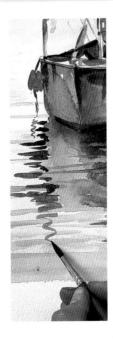

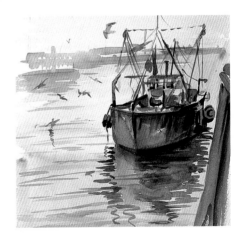

3 *Paint the rigging and masts in diluted black and burnt sienna with a long fine rigger. Paint the gulls with simple brushstrokes at different angles to catch the flurry of activity.*

In context

Both hard and soft edges and brushmarks vary greatly from one artist to another. They all develop individual ways of handling the brush and applying the paint. Artists develop their own characteristic style, just as we develop our own style of handwriting. They also develop preferences for particular kinds of brushes. And this is another factor determining the kinds of brushmarks they are able to make. Each of the artists featured here has a distinctive style of brushwork.

Bridge Series – No. 19

Alex McKibbin

This artist uses a riot of different brushmarks. They seem to skip and dance all over the picture. The effect is very impressionistic, and because a great deal of white paper is left exposed and many bright colors are used, a vivid combination of light and motion is experienced.

The Boat House

Donald Pass

This painting is constructed with many tiny brushmarks. There are washes for the sky, building, and underpainting, but they play a subsidiary role. The lively brushwork is consistent throughout, giving the painting unity. Most of the paint has been applied wet-on-dry, so the strokes have retained their shape.

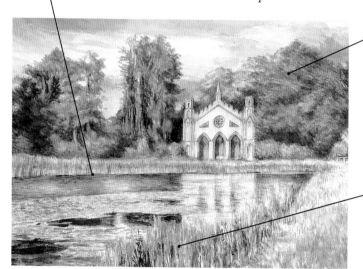

A very fine mesh of delicate horizontal brushstrokes describes the ripples on the surface of the water.

The brushmarks for each tree are applied in a slightly different way to describe their individual characteristics and to provide variety.

The reeds and grasses are rendered with brushmarks at varying angles to indicate the direction of growth.

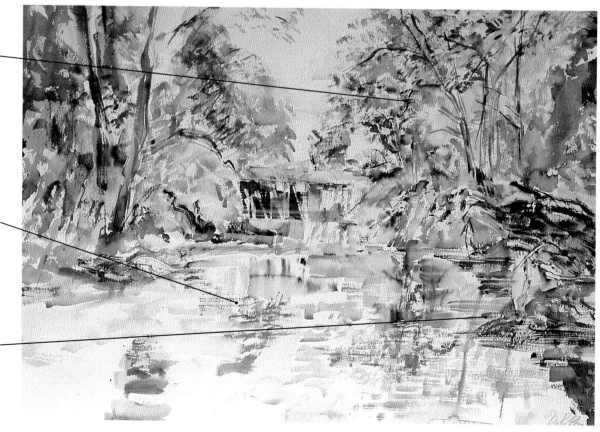

A mixture of colors have been scumbled over a few freehand washes with very dry paint. A complex mosaic of brushmarks was gradually built up.

The water is handled very freely with a mixture of wet and less wet paint. The bright yellow is the reflection of the fall foliage above.

The water surface is described with thick horizontal drybrush strokes. The brush hairs were splayed to form elongated streaks.

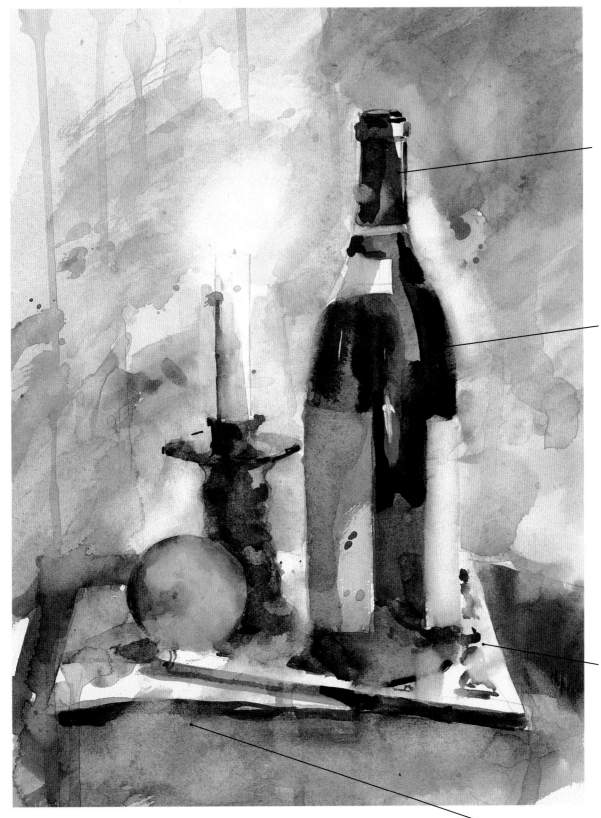

The top of the bottle has been painted with sharp edges. This prevents it from being lost, giving the bottle its shape and solidity.

The shoulders of the bottle are dissolved and softened on either side, which helps to prevent it from overpowering the other objects.

This sharp edge keeps the eye within the picture, leading it back to the bottle.

Still Life With Wine Bottle and Candlestick

John Lidzey

Alternate hard and soft edges can be seen appearing throughout this picture. The simplicity of the still life has allowed the artist a great freedom to express the fluidity of the medium. Solid objects lose their rigidity as they partially soften and merge with their surroundings.

The lower edge is alternately hard and soft, breaking up any horizontal barrier, and drawing the viewer's gaze into the picture.

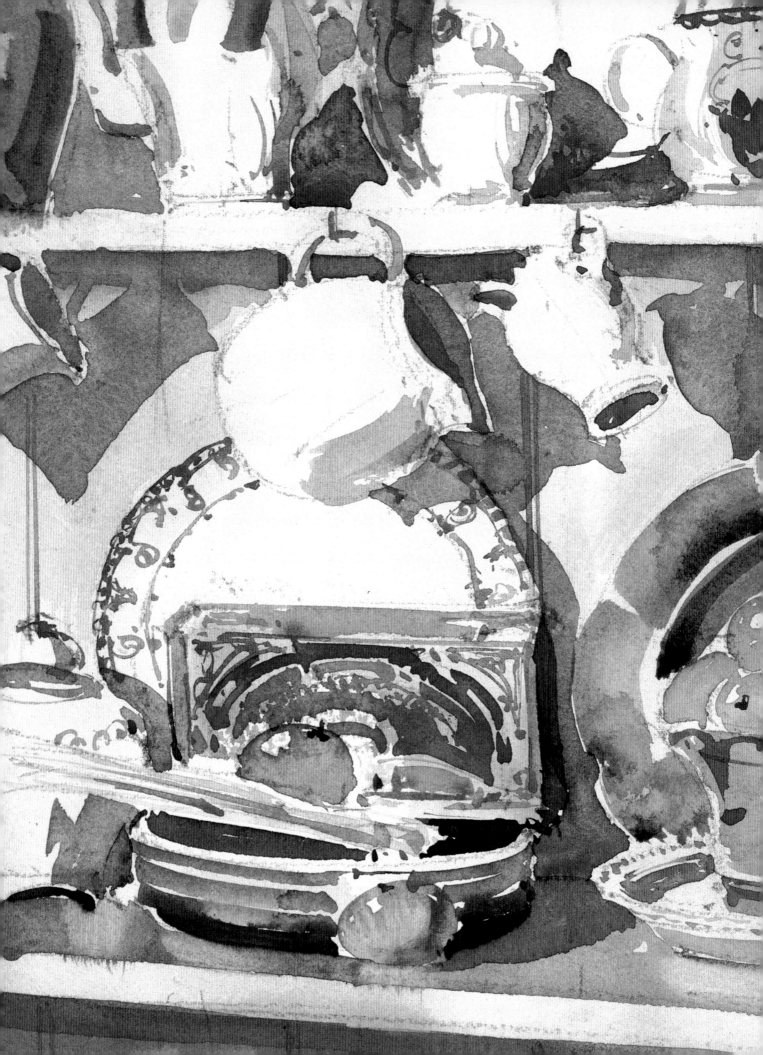

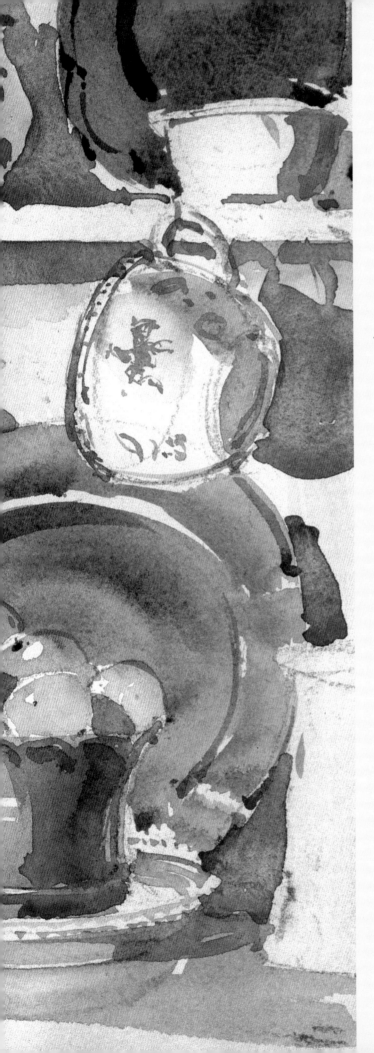

SPECIAL TECHNIQUES

This section looks at special techniques – the watercolor painter's "tricks of the trade." One of the great charms of the medium is it refuses to be completely tamed. Some of the techniques in this section show you how to take advantage of this. Each technique is demonstrated with step-by-step sequences showing its application for a variety of subjects. The demonstrations are backed up by specially chosen and carefully annotated finished paintings which enable you to see how individual artists have adapted the methods to suit their subjects.

Kitchen Still Life
Alan Oliver

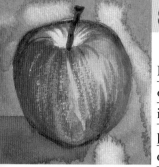

Backruns can occur when painting wet-in-wet (see page 68). As you drop clear water or paint into a damp wash, it doesn't blend in the usual manner but displaces the original color, blooming out and forming a hard-edged irregular puddle. This could ruin an otherwise perfect wash – or be a blessing in disguise.

Backruns

You may sometimes want to create a backrun deliberately to enhance your painting. In this case, lay the initial wash and wait until it's just damp, when the sheen leaves the surface. Then drop in either clear water or fresh paint in large droplets. The surface dampness will act as a vehicle to spread the paint, but it won't be wet enough to merge both layers. After expanding a little, the paint will dry leaving an irregular, hard edge with a concentration of pigment gathered near the outline. If you want to avoid backruns, don't be tempted to add more paint while the wash is drying.

Backruns as texture

Backruns are a particularly useful watercolor technique. Because they give the impression of having formed naturally, they can complement a roughly weathered surface. Though tricky to handle at first, once understood they can be easily controlled by careful timing and by judging the quantity of liquid dropped in accurately, which influences the size to which they grow. Granular pigments respond better than the staining colors.

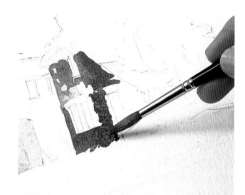

1 **Paint the walls with burnt umber, burnt sienna, yellow ocher, and sap green. After you have laid each area of wash leave it for a couple of minutes. Then charge the brush with either clear water or more paint and touch the spot where you want a backrun to occur with the tip of the brush.**

2 **A number of small backruns can be seen on the walls. These break up the flat washes to give them character and interest. Backruns appear more dramatic on dark washes because larger amounts of pigment are displaced.**

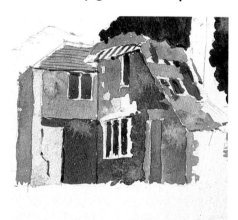

Accidental backruns

1 *After the hair was painted with a mixture of burnt umber and black, a wet brush was allowed to touch the drying paint. This was a mistake and immediately the smooth wash was disrupted with an unintentional backrun.*

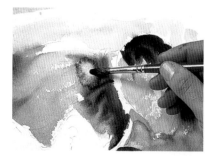

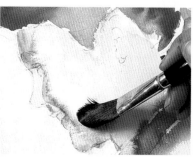

2 *A similar mistake occurred here. First a pale wash of burnt sienna and yellow ocher was applied to the face and one of Venetian red to the shirt. While these areas were still damp, a wet brush was stroked down the cheek to the collar. The original washes were displaced creating an unsightly backrun.*

3 *The backruns in the hair and collar have been effectively worked over to disguise them. The one down the face has been softened a little, but is still visible. Further accidental backruns in the background are acceptable and have been left unaltered.*

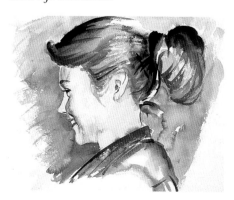

3 Paint the trees with sap green, olive green, burnt umber, and ultramarine. Use burnt sienna and cadmium red light for the chimney. Create backruns in the trees and on the chimney.

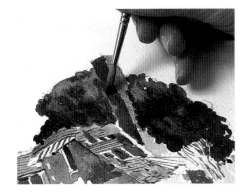

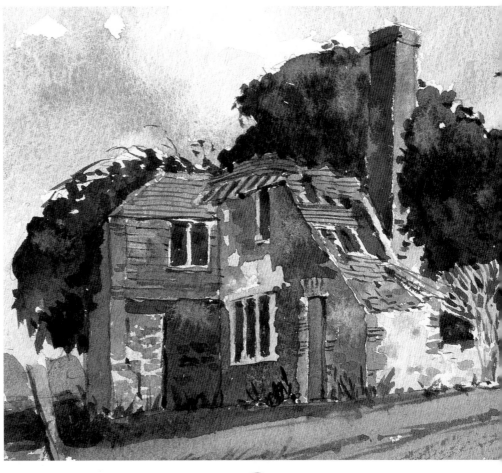

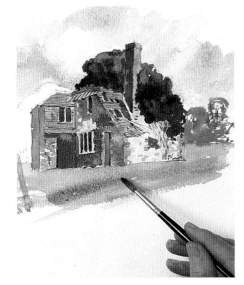

4 Loosely brush the sky with a pale wash of ultramarine and apply a wash of raw sienna over the foreground. Paint the distant trees with sap green mixed with a little raw sienna.

5 The backruns are used here constructively and judiciously to convey variations in color and texture. They are not allowed to overwhelm the overall composition, which is a risk if too much liquid is used.

VARIATION • 2
Unrestrained backruns

I *The billowing smoke from these industrial towers is an ideal opportunity to exploit the irregular features of a backrun. Apply a fluid wash of violet, Venetian red, and black to the left hand part of the sky. Use Naples yellow on the towers and central sky area, with some ultramarine sky breaking through.*

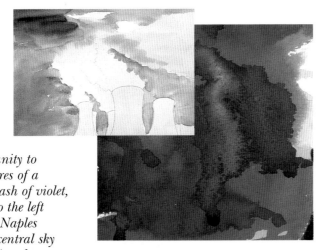

2 *Overlay additional washes of black and ultramarine. To create large flowing backruns make sure the brush contains plenty of fluid.*

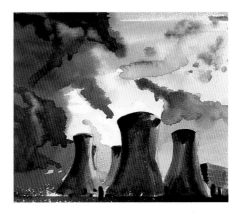

3 *Finish the towers with black, burnt sienna, and Naples yellow. In the completed picture large backruns can be seen in the blue and black smoke, adding to the ominous atmosphere of this scene.*

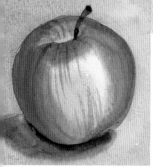

To paint the gradual change of light around a curved object or the blending of two colors takes a substantial amount of control. This delicate procedure creates soft tonal changes on a small scale. It is frequently used for detail in still life, and offers the perfect technique for painting skin tones in portraits.

Blending

When blending colors, speed is important. You will be working into wet paint using little water so that the paint will dry fast, with the risk of an edge forming. To blend one color from dark to light, you have to develop a fairly fast action, laying the darkest tone, rinsing the brush in water, draining the excess water into a tissue, then returning the damp brush to the paper to stroke the still-wet paint, dispersing and blending it. To blend two colors, lay them alongside each other and, with repeated strokes, merge them together. In this case, you won't need to rinse the brush until the end.

Controlling the paint

This painting demonstrates the amount of control possible if you use a medium brush and paint on a dry surface without flooding the surface too much. When the paint is laid it leaves a hard edge, but you can soften this with a clean, damp brush.

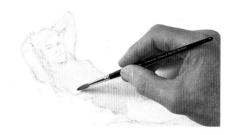

1 **Draw the model's contours,** taking care not to press too hard with the pencil. Mix a little cadmium red light with new gamboge, and lay a soft wash over the figure, omitting the right breast. Clean the brush, shake out excess water, and soften the edge formed around the breast.

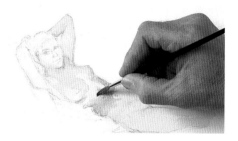

2 **Using a stronger mix of the same colors,** continue modeling the face and torso, carefully blending away hard edges, to create rounded form and gentle curves. Always use a little paint to keep full control.

VARIATION • 1
Fusion of colors

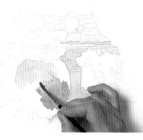

1 *Paint the urn in the foreground by laying yellow ocher at the top with a little cerulean blue. Then paint burnt sienna at the bottom. Carefully blend the colors together by stroking sideways with a clean, wet brush where they meet. Repeat for the smaller urn.*

2 *Paint the background with flat washes, keeping within the pencil guidelines. To prevent two colors bleeding into one another while one is drying, move around the picture. Use mixtures of yellow ocher, Hooker's green, alizarin crimson, and cerulean blue. Add further layers of color to suggest detail.*

3 *In the finished picture, everything serves to emphasize the large urn. The trees and flowers frame and focus the eye on the urn. The background urn echoes its larger counterpart. The gently curving surface of the urn is prominent and contrasts with the muted flat, gray washes behind.*

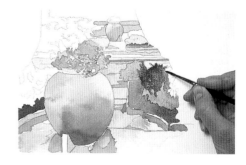

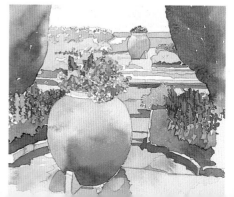

3 Follow the same procedure down the legs. Apply paint down either side of each leg, then soften the edges down the inside, leaving a lighter tone down the middle. This will convey the rounded form of the leg.

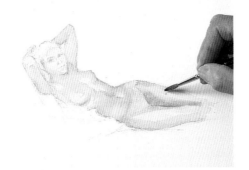

4 Paint the hair with ultramarine and burnt umber. Add more concentrated skin tones to accentuate the form further. Use deeper tones in the most recessed areas. Continue along the arms, the top edge of the body, and around the abdomen.

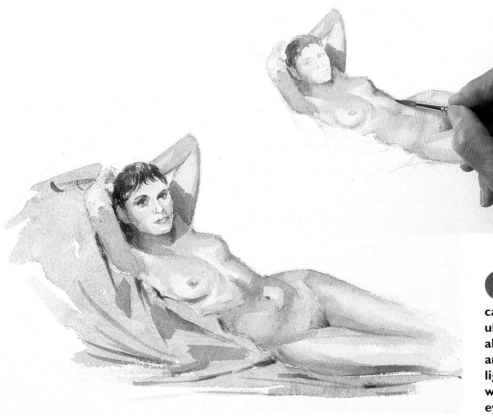

5 Paint the fabric with cerulean blue mixed with cadmium red light. Use ultramarine for the creases. Add in all the remaining details of the face and the body. Use cadmium red light for the lips, and ultramarine with cadmium red light for the eyes and brows.

VARIATION • 2
Merging overlapping colors

1 *Lay a wet-on-dry Winsor yellow wash on each apple, with greater concentration on the left-hand sides. Allow to dry completely. Paint around the right side of the apple at the rear with cadmium red, following the contours of the apple in front. Use clean water to soften and blend.*

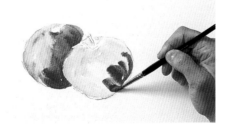

2 *Repeat the process with the second apple, making it appear slightly different from the first. Add a little ultramarine and Venetian red into the red areas of both apples to darken the right sides and create a three-dimensional effect.*

3 *Paint the stalks and tips of the apples with sepia. Darken the base of both apples to increase the sense of three-dimensional solidity.*

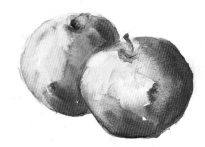

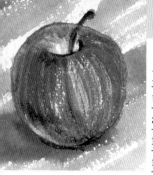

Most watercolor techniques take advantage of the fluidity of the medium; this technique provides a counter-balance by exploiting the medium's dryness. Observe how a sweeping brush stroke unloads its paint and gradually breaks into a sparkling stream of fragmented color. The rough paper surface plays an important part in this process as the paint becomes too dry to fill the valleys.

Dry-brush

Dry-brush, which may at first appear a haphazard method, can, when fully mastered, become a wonderfully expressive addition to the family of watercolor techniques. The basic principle to understand is that insufficient or thick, sticky paint combined with a relatively fast arm action will cause the brushstroke gradually to disintegrate. Dragging the side of the brush greatly helps. If there is excess fluid, you can squeeze this out of the brush with your fingers. To vary the effect, you can splay the brush hairs out with your fingers whilst painting, and reducing the downward pressure on the brush during the stroke will produce a more fragmented effect.

Dry-brush as texture

Dry-brush is used here specifically to portray a harsh, rugged environment. It has a dual function as texture for the snow-clad mountain and also to impart the sensation of movement as cold wind lashes the grass. The latter effect is achieved with broken, diagonal strokes for the grass.

1 To convey the heavy, foreboding sky, wet the sky area with a large squirrel-hair brush. Using sweeping, horizontal strokes, drop in strong solutions of first Payne's gray then black. Allow them to bleed together and spread in different directions.

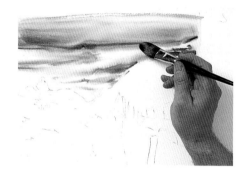

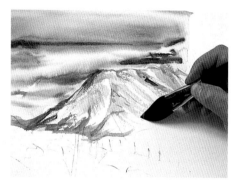

2 When the sky has dried, barely dampen the brush with a mix of violet and black. With light, downward strokes and holding the brush at an angle, paint the side of the mountain. Skim the paper surface so that the brushstrokes break up.

VARIATION • I
Dry-brush highlights

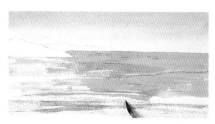

1 *Paint a gradated wash of cobalt blue and lemon yellow in the sky. Mix violet with cobalt blue for the sea, and Vandyke brown with violet for the foreground. Paint wet brushstrokes on the right side of the picture and dry-brush on the left half.*

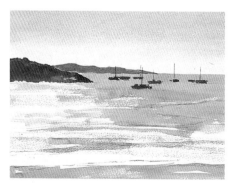

2 *Mix neutral tint with ultramarine for the shoreline and yachts. You can now see how the dry-brush technique is perfect for representing the sparkling water surface as the low sun reflects over calm sea and wet sand.*

3 *Mix a fairly thick solution of neutral tint and, using the side of a No. 10 brush, skim long, horizontal strokes over the beach area to build up the rich texture of the foreground.*

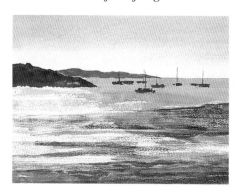

3 Paint a band of Payne's gray above the mountain and the middle-distance hills. Lay a pale black wash over the foreground and leave to dry. With a just-damp brush, paint diagonal strokes in burnt sienna and Vandyke brown for the grass. Keep all these strokes at approximately the same angle.

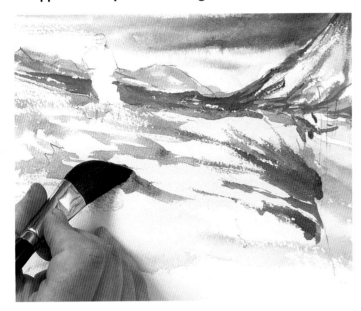

4 Paint over the grass with black dry-brush strokes. Use some wetter, curved strokes to suggest the shape of the snow mounds on the ground.

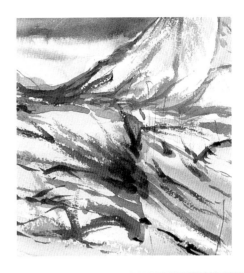

5 Finally, add the main points of interest – the fence with its curved perspective, diminishing in size to describe the slope falling away, and the figure, painted in Vandyke brown, black, and gray.

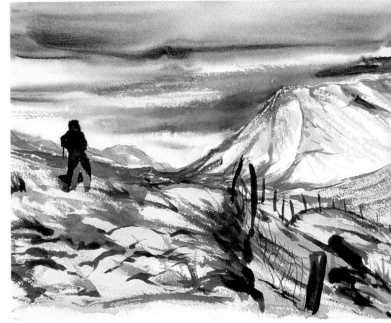

VARIATION • 2
Simple and dynamic dry-brush

1 *Paint the sky with a wash of raw umber and cobalt blue. While still damp, paint two dark clumps of shrub on the horizon with ultramarine and burnt umber. When dry, take a No. 4 brush with a little of the same color, and add some dry streaks upward from the left shrub.*

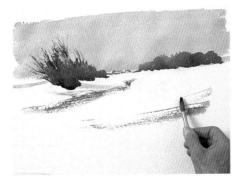

2 *Using the side of the brush, skim dry mixtures of olive green, ultramarine, and raw umber across the snow. With a thick mixture of the same colors, start to block in the body of the foreground shrub.*

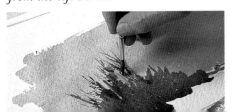

3 *Extend dry strokes upward from the foreground shrub. Finally, paint in the receding fence posts and the grass at the base with burnt umber and ultramarine. As they recede, make them paler and smaller.*

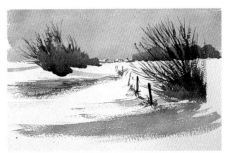

In context

The use of dry brush, blending, and backruns is demonstrated in the finished paintings on these pages. These techniques can be easily distinguished as they contribute to a combined effect, like the individual notes played in a concert.

Back Street, Funchal, Madeira

Colin Radcliffe

The balance between the use of dry-brush and wet-in-wet and wet-in-dry is just about perfect in this painting. The dry-brush is used in a descriptive role to indicate the textural qualities of the old building, and as a compositional tool in contrast to the soft blending. The painting is largely about the play of light. The dry-brush work plays an important role in emphasizing contrasts.

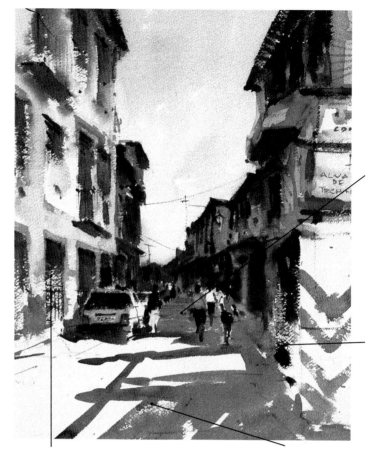

The central area is treated very differently, using mainly wet-in-wet brushwork, and very dark paint. A diffused effect in the deep shadow areas is designed to stir the imagination.

The right side of the street is in deeper shade, with less opportunity for dry-brush work, but this strong dry-brush stroke where the light meets the shade is crucial in balancing the extensive dry-brush work on the left.

Dry-brush is painted in a single downward stroke, with fairly thick paint, for each window and door, giving the building character and surface texture.

A little dry-brush work is carefully used on the road, where the shadow is close to the bright reflected light. This suggests the reflection of light on the rough texture of the road surface.

The Swimming Lesson

Henry W. Dixon

This masterly painting has used blending as a modeling tool extensively. The excitement and activity have been captured by the accurate representation of the children's features. Blending helps to create three dimensional quality.

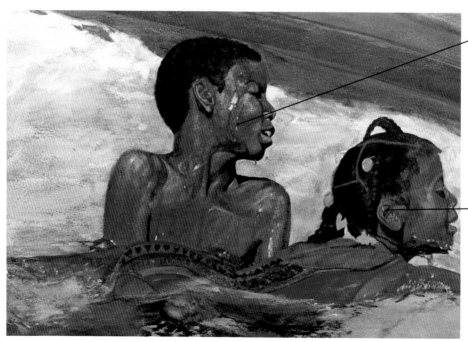

Careful manipulation of tones has produced gentle curves for the cheek, neck, and shoulders. The forms are enhanced by the build-up of several blended glazes.

The girl's ear and features show very intricate blending and modeling. This detail was accomplished with a very fine brush and careful study of the subjects.

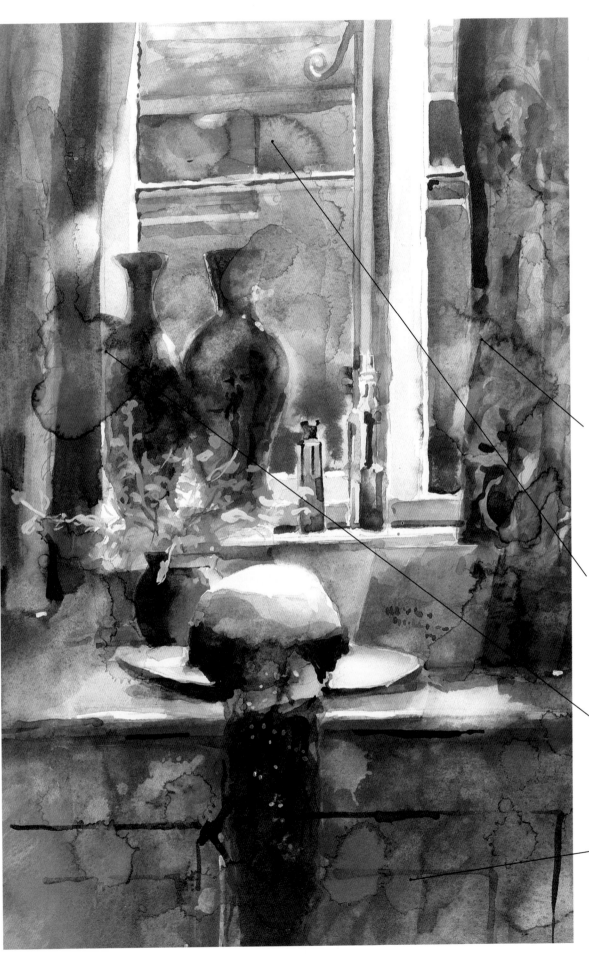

Interior With Hat

John Lidzey

This artist has cleverly incorporated backruns into the composition. Used in this way, they are exciting and natural, forming interesting flowery patterns wherever they appear. The general style of the painting is extremely accurate, but there is also a sense of spontaneity where backruns have been allowed to occur.

This large backrun crosses several verticals and forms a large, irregular puddle, partially dissolving some hard edges.

Beautifully aligned with the centers of interest, this small backrun is very clear. It adds interest to an area which otherwise could be plain.

The strong verticals of the drape are softened by this large backrun, which links the vase and the drape, setting up an interplay between the separate areas.

The lower part of the picture is filled with numerous small backruns. These provide interest and freshness, maintaining a sense of activity over the entire picture area.

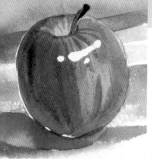

You will find that you often have to paint round awkward shapes, creating patchy brushmarks as you follow the difficult edges. If you mask the shapes out first, then you can paint over them, liberating the brush to paint a smooth background.

Masking Fluid

Masking fluid is ideally suited to the watercolorist; it's a rubber solution which, when applied quickly dries in contact with air, perfectly sealing the paper. Moreover, when it is dry, you can easily rub if off with your finger or with a ball of dried masking fluid. Take care not to leave masking fluid on for more than a day, or it could tear the paper when you rub it off. To clean the brush during use, stir it in concentrated dishwashing (washing-up) liquid, then rinse in warm water. To remove more stubborn rubber, soak temporarily denatured alcohol (white spirit), then comb out with a tooth brush.

Painting on masking fluid

It is tempting to use an old brush for painting masking fluid, as this clogs brushes quickly and they need stern cleaning methods. However, it is best to use a good, fine brush with this fiddly subject or the spots of sunlight will appear as awkward shapes.

1 Make a preliminary pencil sketch that notes the position of any highlights. Apply a pale wash of cadmium red all over the areas on which highlights are planned. Dry this thoroughly – with a hairdryer, if necessary. Use a soft No. 2 brush to reserve all the highlights with neat masking fluid. Allow it to dry.

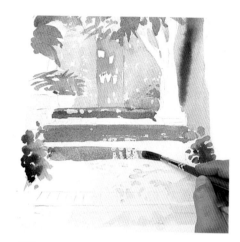

2 Continue to build up the picture with progressively darker washes of sap green, ultramarine, burnt sienna, Payne's gray, and violet. Notice how the dried masking fluid displaces the paint, and shows up as yellow blobs.

VARIATION • I
Spattering masking fluid

I *For this painting masking fluid is applied in two consecutive layers. Apply an initial wash of pale burnt sienna. Allow to dry completely, then* 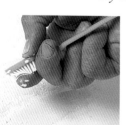 *spatter on some masking fluid by loading a toothbrush and flicking the bristles with a finger.*

2 *Paint a second wash over the dried masking fluid, reserving the shapes of the figures. When this is dry, rub off the masking fluid and spatter on a second layer, creating larger blobs as well as a fine spray. Cover almost half the surface and allow the fluid to dry.*

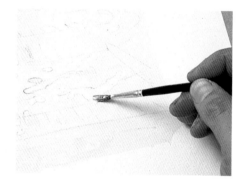

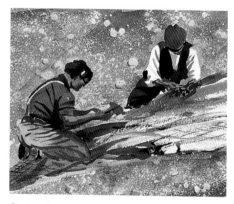

3 *Apply a third wash – a darker combination of burnt sienna and violet. When dry, rub off the second layer of masking fluid. Finish painting the two fishermen mending their nets using the same limited palette with the addition of black and ultramarine.*

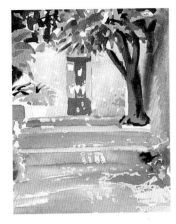

3 Paint the tree trunk with burnt umber and violet. Then add indigo along the dark side of the trunk and to the darkest leaves.

4 When all the paint is completely dry, you can start to rub off the masking fluid. Any wet paint will smudge. You will need to rub all over in case you miss any small areas of masking fluid. Using a clean finger, first skim over the large areas, breaking up the surface. Then rub little by little, being careful not to tear the paper.

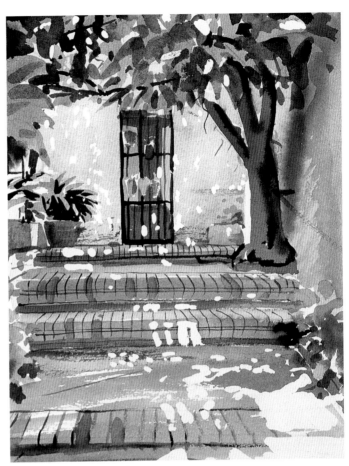

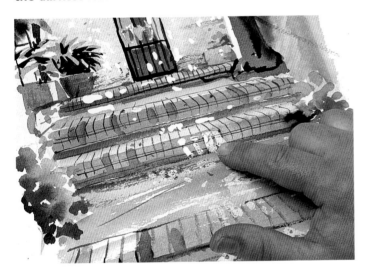

5 After you have rubbed off all of the masking fluid, brush off the bits with a large cloth or kitchen paper. The initial red wash, although pale, makes a significant difference to the highlights now exposed.

VARIATION • 2
Rubbing masking fluid

1 *Paint the sea and the seagull. Paint a pale, variegated wash on the wooden breaker. Allow to dry. Cover the breakers with a film of masking fluid. When that is dry, partially rub it off and overpaint with Vandyke brown.*

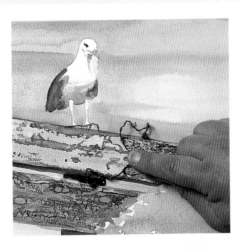

2 *When the paint is dry, rub off the remaining masking fluid. This reveals a rough texture where the brown paint has found its way through the partially rubbed film.*

3 *Complete the painting by adding detail to the seagull, suggesting wood grain on the breakers, and giving form to the pebbles. Finally paint the rusty bolt in the center of the breaker.*

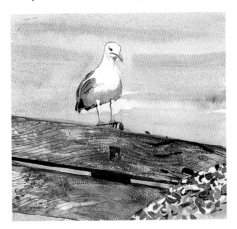

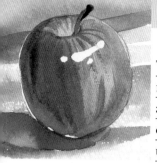

To mask a rectangle accurately, or to enable you to paint up against a long straight edge, it's easiest to use masking tape. For an irregular shape resembling the tree-line on the horizon, you can use the torn edge of a sheet of paper.

Using Masks

With its qualities of low adhesion and ease of cutting, masking tape is tailor-made for the job of masking. You can lay down whole strips to mask the edge of large buildings, or parallel overlapping strips to cover large areas. Alternatively, you can cut out shapes from it to make stencils. The thicker the paint you are using, the less likely it is to bleed under the tape. Brush it on in one clean stroke, and leave to dry before stripping off the tape. To make an irregular edge, secure a torn paper edge in position with tape. Then paint over and away from the torn edge so that paint isn't forced underneath.

Cutting masks

Most masking tapes are semi-transparent so when you lay them over a drawing you can see through them sufficiently to cut out the shape you wish to mask. Take care when cutting not to score into the paper or it may tear when you pull off the mask. One advantage tape has over masking fluid is that it's easier to get accurate straight lines with freehand cutting or, if necessary, with a ruler.

1 Draw the outlines of the object you wish to mask slightly darker than usual. Lay the masking tape in strips over it to cover the complete shape. Using a scalpel, and with a steady hand, cut through the tape around the shape. Be careful not to cut the paper.

2 Peel away the superfluous tape. For small enclosed areas carefully lift up a corner with the scalpel, then peel off. Press down the remaining tape in case it has lifted in the process.

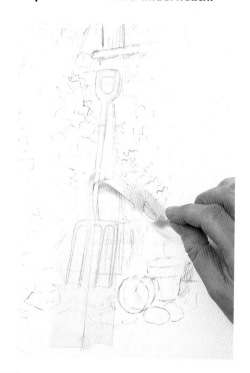

VARIATION • I
Masking straight edges

1 *Cover the roof with a strip of masking tape and trim to match the roof's outline. Add a little extra tape for the chimney. Brushing the paint over the tape, paint the countryside with Winsor blue, cerulean blue, and yellow ocher. Add a little alizarin crimson to the mountain. Use Payne's gray for the fence, road, and rear rooftop. Paint the detail of the door and windows.*

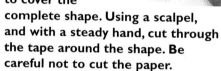

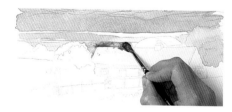

2 *When the paint is thoroughly dry, carefully peel off the tape.*

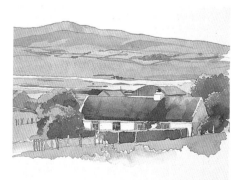

3 *Paint the roof with magenta and a little of the previous mix of green. The accuracy of the masking has given the cottage a solidity, in contrast to the gentle curves of its surroundings.*

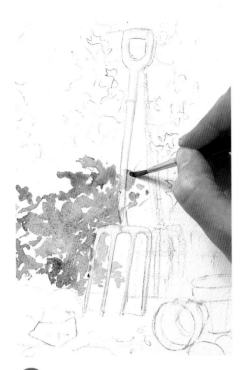

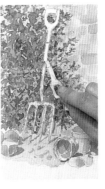

4 Finish the foliage, adding a little Prussian blue. When all the paint is completely dry, peel off the mask. Do this slowly to avoid tearing.

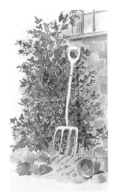

5 If there are any pencil lines visible inside the fork, rub these off. The way the paint has been applied has helped to prevent any seeping under the tape, so you have a perfectly clean edge.

3 Using Hooker's green dark, freely paint the leaves, taking your brushmarks over the masking tape. Use light red and burnt umber for the wall and pots, cerulean blue on the window, and Payne's gray for the paving. Use Winsor violet for the shadow under the fork. Build up using small washes.

6 Use a No. I brush to complete the fork detail in cerulean blue and burnt umber. This will prevent its looking like a cut-out. The shadow behind the fork is important because it links it with the background.

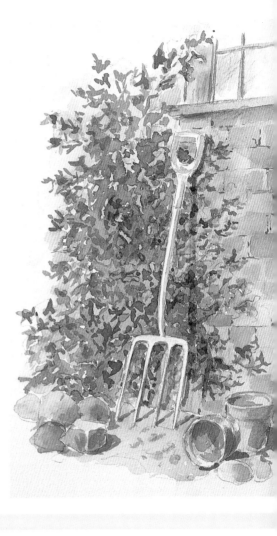

VARIATION · 2
Torn paper mask

I *Blotting paper makes an excellent freehand mask. It tears with a serrated edge, and prevents water seeping underneath by absorbing it. Tear it to shape, lay it in position, and brush paint onto a dry picture surface across and away from the torn edge so you don't force paint underneath.*

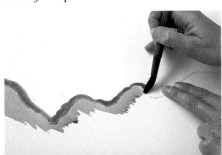

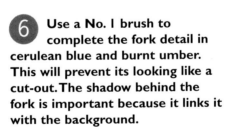

2 *When you have established the outline of the mountains, fill in the sky with Payne's gray and Antwerp blue. Lift the mask carefully to avoid smudging the wet paint.*

3 *Dampen the surface of the mountains and apply strokes of Payne's gray. Add some darker gray to the right side of the peaks. The end result is simple but effective, giving to the mountains a rocky, three-dimensional appearance.*

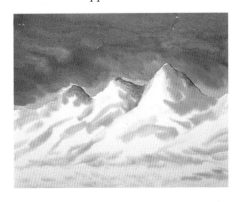

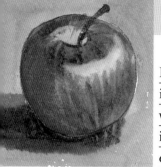

Lifting out is an integral part of watercolor painting technique. It's easy to lay down excessive color or too much water, in which case you will need to soak up the excess. Lifting out can also be useful for "negative painting," for example, lifting an object such as a cloud out of the painted surface is more effective than trying to paint around it.

Lifting out

A "thirsty" brush, sponge, cotton buds, blotting paper, absorbent cloth, and facial tissues all make excellent lifting-out tools. Lifting out of a wet surface requires quick reactions, however, so have the tools ready. To soak up paint from a wet surface, dab with a tissue before the paint has had time to soak in. By crumpling the tissue, you can get interesting textures. A thirsty brush (one that's clean and dry enough to soak up water) will lift lines out of a damp surface. Blotting paper is as effective as tissue, and creates marvelous textures. On a dry surface, scrub with a bristle brush then dab with tissue.

Lifting out when dry

In order to lift off paint effectively, this scene has to be overpainted using excessive paint. This will allow plenty of scope to get back to white paper, revealing plenty of contrast. Take care not to overdo the application since this can have a deadening effect.

1 Paint the bright background areas with Indian yellow. Then paint the tree trunks in Vandyke brown, and the shaded foreground leaves in olive green, terre verte, and cobalt blue. The long foreground shadows and yellow background give the impression of backlit trees.

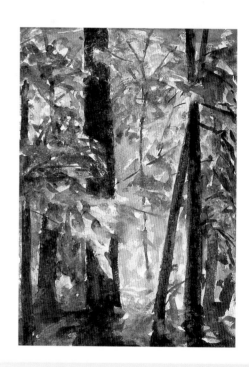

VARIATION • I
Lifting out of a wet surface

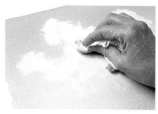

I *Lay a gradated wash of Antwerp blue, making it darker at the top and paler at the bottom. Holding a crumpled tissue, press down firmly in the cloud area to dab off the paint. This will expose almost perfectly white paper.*

2 *When this has dried, add a little Payne's gray into the white area. This time coil the tissue to a point, and lift off the color around the edges of the gray. This exposes the silver lining of the backlit cloud.*

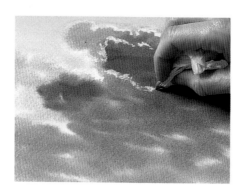

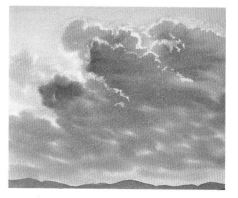

3 *Paint the distant hills in dilute Payne's gray, then add a strip of more concentrated color for the foreground.*

2 Use a moist, short-hair bristle brush and a thin, metal template to reveal light rays with clean sharp edges. Work gradually without too much pressure, so the paper surface isn't unnecessarily roughened. Then mop up the excess residue with tissue.

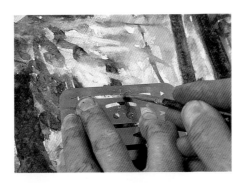

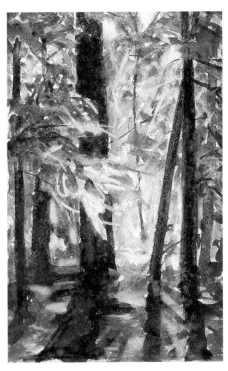

3 To remove large areas without sharp edges, work over the paper freehand with the brush. The brush should be slightly wetter than in the previous step in order to dampen the surface and dislodge more of the pigment.

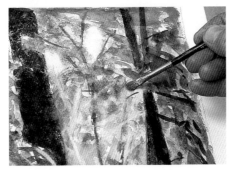

4 While the surface is still damp, hold a piece of tissue in a tight wad and dab it on the surface, picking up the paint residue without leaving any unwanted texture. Do this gently: a wet paper surface is more vulnerable to damage.

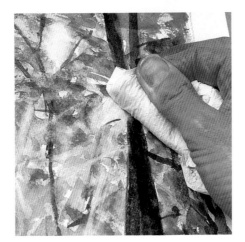

5 The finished picture is light and airy, with rays of sunshine breaking through the trees. The sharp contrast between the darkest trunk and the light area in the center of the picture makes these rays appear intensely bright.

VARIATION • 2
Lifting off with blotting paper

1 *The aim is to partially lift off the paint, leaving a texture on the ground. Paint the woods in Indian yellow, olive green, cadmium red, and Vandyke brown. Then lay a wash of Winsor violet and Vandyke brown on the ground.*

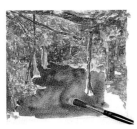

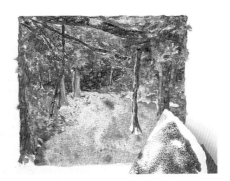

2 *Paint the ground with a more concentrated mix of the same colors. Lay the blotting paper over it and stroke it gently with your hand, not pressing too hard, to remove some of the paint on the surface. Carefully peel off the blotting paper.*

3 *Spray the trees with an atomizer for an effect that corresponds nicely with the texture on the ground. If necessary, repeat the blotting paper technique on the ground to build up more texture, or simply paint over it with a few well-placed brushstrokes.*

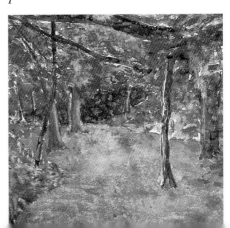

In context

Masking and lifting out are related techniques, that both seek to retain the paper surface or previous paint in specific areas. The two paintings on this page provide extensive examples of masking. Masking fluid has been used as a constructional tool in the process of building up over several layers.

Once all the areas to be reserved had been protected with masking fluid, this variegated background wash was applied.

Garden Party

Judi Betts

Masking fluid is used extensively here in order to permit the use of a series of fresh, unhindered washes, which result in a light, airy painting. The number of glazes was kept to a minimum, so that even the darkest areas sing with light as the paper shines through.

After the masking fluid was removed from these background highlights, each one was carefully filled with bright colors in a highly decorative way.

The masking fluid on this part of the chair was removed last. The white paper exposed is one of the brightest areas and provides a good counterpoint to the dark area behind.

There is evidence here of two stages of masking. The first stage has already been painted in, leaving the second stage as white highlights.

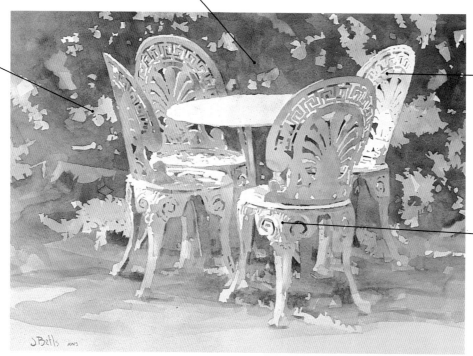

Beaverdam Swamp II

Mary Ann Pope

This painting has been masked in several stages, building up a complex picture of overlapping masking. Most of the detail was established when the masking was applied, only needing to be filled in later. The painting is a remarkable achievement of masking, in methodical stages.

The background wash of light and dark greens can be seen to be continuous across the top of the picture. All the tree trunks and foliage were masked out together.

The diagonal warm yellow areas and leaves floating on the surface remained masked throughout the painting and were only filled in with color at the end.

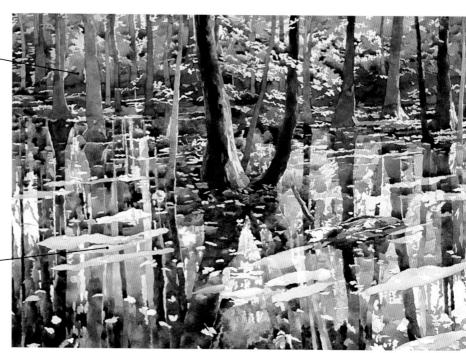

Evening, Wacton Common, Norfolk

Maurice Read

The large sky area is the most dramatic and eye-catching feature of this painting. The soft, wispy clouds were made by lifting paint out of the damp surface with a thirsty brush, cotton bud or a tightly coiled piece of tissue. A pointed instrument was used to make the fine marks. The use of cobalt blue makes lifting out more effective, as it is a granular paint that is easy to dislodge.

Lifting out the clouds has produced a soft effect that is easy to control. Although this is best done when wet, it can also be achieved when dry using a hard eraser.

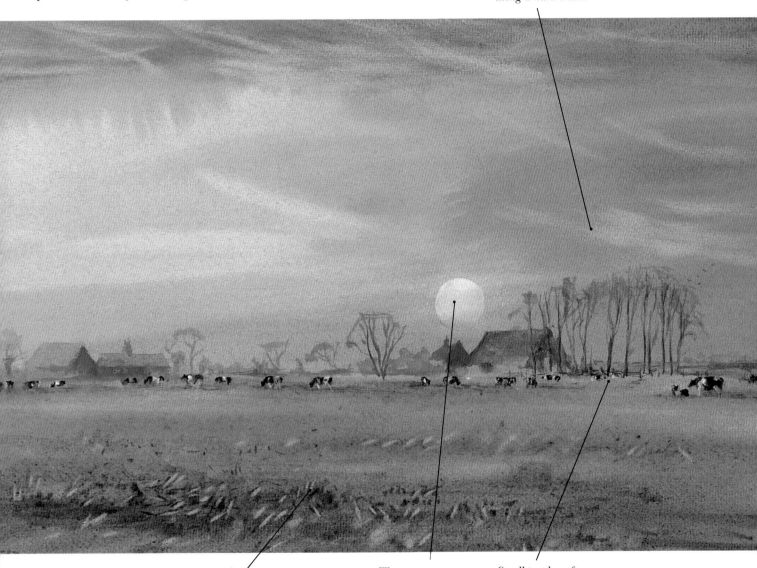

The small diagonal strokes have been lifted out of the dry surface with an eraser and a straight edge.

The sun was accurately drawn with a circular template and masked to protect it from the sky wash.

Small touches of white body color have been used to suggest the individual cows. It has been applied with quick flicks of the brush.

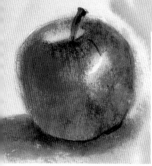

Scumbling is a close relative of dry-brush (see page 86) and a valuable textural technique, resembling a nicely weathered surface. The uneven, feathery marks produced leave much paper showing through, which means that you can superimpose several layers. The technique generally produces a fine grain which is specially suitable for transient, hazy, atmospheric effects such as the shimmering light around a lamp-post.

Scumbling

Scumbling is a good way to use old brushes, particularly bristle brushes which can take plenty of punishment – you may not want to use your new sable ones. Instead of dragging the brush across the paper, apply downward pressure and work in a circular motion, taking advantage of the rough paper surface. The hairs of the brush will splay out making many fine, circular marks. If the paint is too wet the effect will be lost, as the color will start to blend and soak away, so both paint and surface must be dry. By mixing watercolor with gum arabic (see **Liquid Aids**, page 138) and not water, you will get the right consistency.

Scumbling single color

The unique texture created by scumbling will contrast with surrounding washes, giving maximum impact to the bell tower. The paint must be very thick. Use your oldest, roughest, bristle brush for scumbling. Don't apply the technique until you have finished the rest of your picture.

1 Paint the sky with a wash of cobalt blue and a little manganese blue near the bottom. Mix Indian red with a little violet for the shaded building on the right.

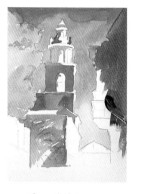

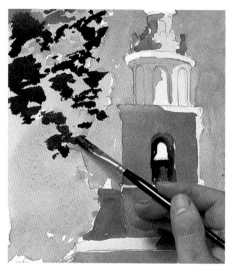

2 Paint the foliage with variegated washes of cadmium yellow and sap green. Use violet and ultramarine on the bell tower. Apply a mix of sap green with a little black using a ⅜ inch (1 cm) long, flat brush for the darker leaves on the tree.

VARIATION • 1
Scumble build-up

1 *Build up the picture over the drawing, using ultramarine for the sky, burnt sienna and burnt umber for the ruins, and Hooker's green dark with yellow ocher for the grass. Scumble successive layers of Payne's gray, burnt umber, and burnt sienna over the ruined wall in the foreground.*

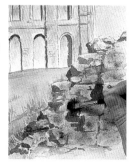

2 *Mix cerulean blue with Chinese white and scumble over the previous layers. This is a more opaque mix than the earlier colors, but allows the original dark scumbles to show through the pale blue texture.*

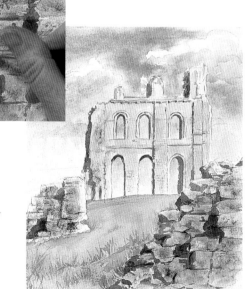

3 *Repeat the scumbling process, but with a lighter touch and excluding the pale blue, on the left-hand rocks. Scumble a small amount of burnt sienna onto the distant ruin: its fine texture won't be so visible at a distance.*

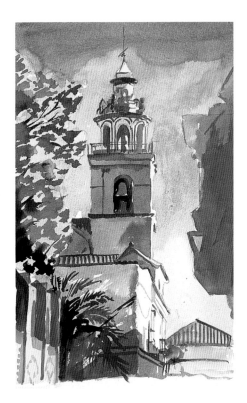

3 With a No. 4 brush, put in all the detail on the bell tower, bottom left wall, shadows on palm tree, etc., using combinations of ultramarine, black, burnt umber, and burnt sienna.

4 Make sure that the bell tower is dry. With an old bristle brush, pick up some thick, concentrated black paint; you can add some gum arabic to soften the color if needed. Press down onto the paper surface, splaying the hairs and scrubbing in small circular motions.

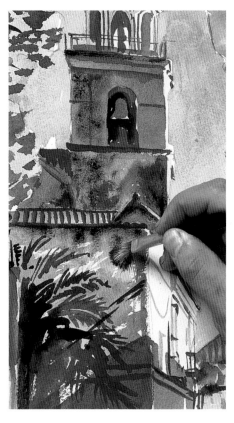

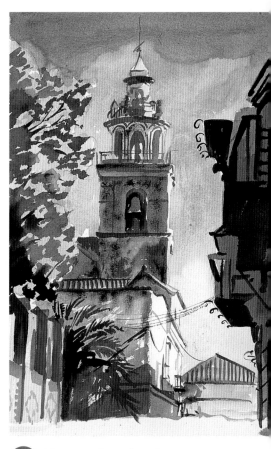

5 To complete the picture, paint black detail on the shaded building on the right. Add the telephone cables with a No. 0 brush. Although the tower appears central in this composition, it is actually slightly left of center which is most effective.

VARIATION · 2
Thick scumble

1 *Prepare the basic painting with broad, sideways strokes at varying angles, allowing some of the paper to break through. Use mixes of violet, Prussian blue, and Payne's gray. Paint the hedgerows in Payne's gray. When dry, scumble over the hedges with a thick mix of Payne's gray.*

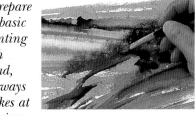

2 *Continue scumbling around the banks of the pond, using a circular motion while pressing down and jabbing motions to force the paint down into the grain. Working in this way creates a soft, irregular texture.*

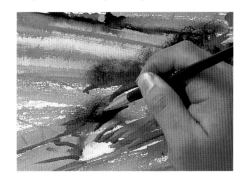

3 *Using a fine brush, paint in the the tufts of grass in the foreground. Dry-brush some Payne's gray onto the foreground, which will re-emphasize the sloping, ploughed field.*

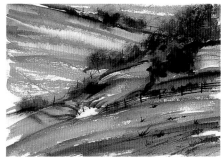

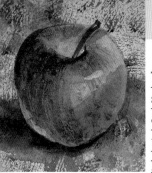

Textures 1

This is a broad subject that can only be touched upon here, and your aim should be to experiment to see the different textures you can produce. There are many ways to apply paint other than the standard methods, each creating a different effect. The knack is to use a texture so that it successfully creates the illusion of natural phenomena.

There are several ways you can produce texture, for example: adding grainy substances such as salt, to the paint; imprinting—transferring paint from a textured surface to the paper; altering the paper's surface texture with textured paste; applying paint with materials other than brushes, including rags, mesh or netting; using abrasive techniques such as sandpaper; stamping—making marks with found objects; and so on. Most texture techniques work better on a dry surface, particularly sandpaper, but some, such as salt, are more effective wet. Practice all these methods on rough paper first as they are unpredictable, and each has special properties that you need to discover. Learn how they can mimic nature, introducing a new sense of realism.

Textured paste

Textured paste can be bought either readymade in jars or you can make it yourself by adding fine sand or polyfilla to acrylic gel or white glue. Once dried, like acrylic paint, it will not dissolve when painted over. You can manipulate textured paste with a palette knife or toothbrush to form a wide variety of surface textures.

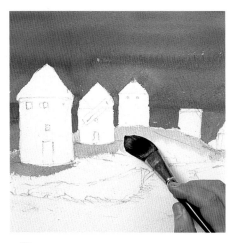

1 Paint the sky with a broad wash of ultramarine and violet. Use Venetian red and violet for the far land and burnt sienna for the foreground.

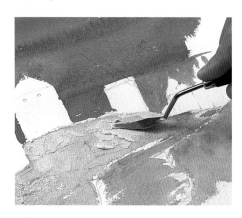

2 Using a painting knife, smear the textured paste thickly on the foreground hill. Then add a thin layer to the right of each windmill. Move it over the paper surface to resemble areas of sand and rock and allow to dry.

VARIATION • 1
Salt

1 *As you finish applying the wash for each area sprinkle* 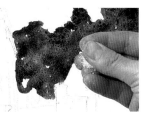 *some coarse sea salt into the wet paint. Use greater quantities of water in each wash than usual to give the salt longer to act. First lay a strong mix of black, violet, ultramarine, and olive green on the trees.*

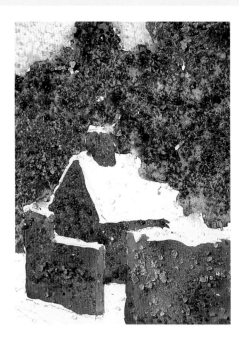

2 *Paint the sky yellow ocher and sprinkle on some salt. Apply burnt umber with Venetian red and a little black to the house, again followed by salt.*

3 *As you complete each area of the row of houses on the left, sprinkle a few grains of salt into the wet paint.*

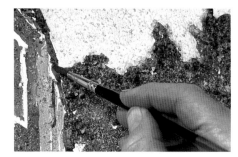

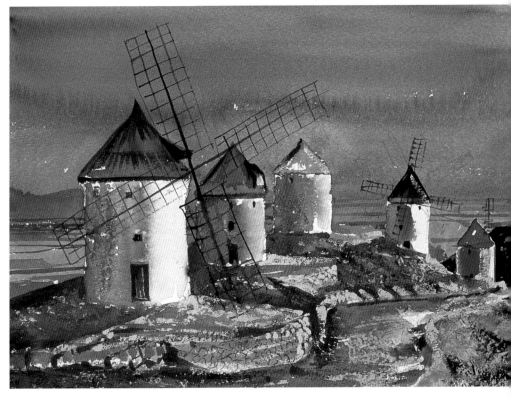

3 Brush fairly thick burnt sienna over the hillside, skimming over the textured parts to allow the naturally gritty texture to show through.

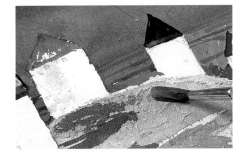

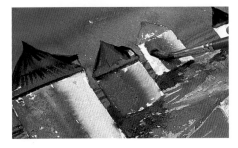

4 From left to right paint horizontal strips of Naples yellow, violet, and ultramarine on the walls of the windmills.

5 Work a third, thicker coat of sepia and ultramarine over the hillside for the areas in shade. Use Payne's gray, burnt sienna, and ultramarine on the road. Skim some Naples yellow body color over the parts of the hillside that are catching the low sunlight. Paint in the sails of the windmills and the windows with a rigger. The textured paste contributes significantly to the successful portrayal of the rugged landscape of La Mancha in central Spain.

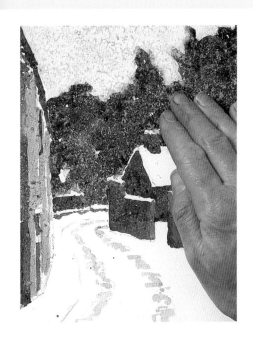

4 *Salt is a water-soluble crystal that gradually dissolves and displaces the paint that immediately surrounds it, creating intricate flowery patterns. This is a slow process, so leave plenty of time. It takes up to 20 minutes to dry thoroughly, after which you can gently rub it off with your fingers.*

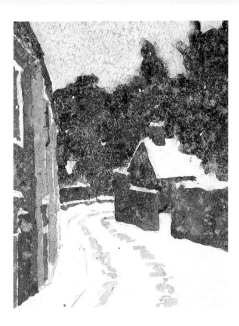

5 *The result is a mysterious effect where the texture resembles snow crystals giving a distinctly wintry feeling. Little detail is necessary, as it would detract from the effect.*

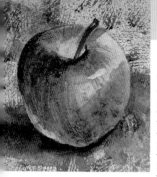

This is the domain of special effects where the normal rules are relaxed, and the powers of the imagination are stretched. Some texture-making techniques are ideally suited to convey particular objects, such as salt crystals for snowflakes or lichen on rocks. Often the technique will represent a surface that has its own, actual texture, such as the bark of a tree or the surface of a stone.

Using plastic wrap

Try out this technique on a scrap piece of the same paper you will use in the painting. Your first attempt does carry a high risk of failure, but remember that you can always turn the paper over and try again.

Textures 2

Before you start painting, make sure you have all the accessories at hand, so as not to interrupt your momentum once you begin. I keep a collection of tried and tested materials in a carton close to the drawing board, as this kind of work is usually confined to the studio due to the quantity of materials involved. My collection includes fine and coarse sandpaper, plastic wrap (cling film), foil, etc. I also use a roller for pressing imprints. Natural objects, for instance, leaves, feathers or stones, print unique shapes.

1 Lay a generous wash of burnt umber mixed with raw sienna on the road area. Then place a large piece of plastic wrap (cling film) over the wash. Brush over it with the side of your hand to produce crinkles. Leave in place for a few minutes.

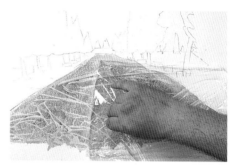

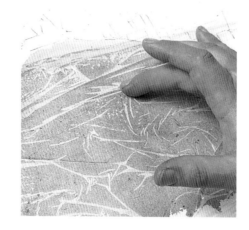

2 Peel off the plastic wrap before the paint is completely dry. If the pattern is successful, you can hasten the drying with a hairdryer. (Don't put the plastic wrap back on.)

VARIATION • 1
Sandpaper

1 *Paint the sky with washes of cobalt blue, and dry-brush the sand with Naples yellow and burnt sienna. Paint the boat with layers of burnt sienna, Indian red, cobalt blue, and raw umber. Overpaint thick black bands on the hull. Build up the boat's shadow with glazes of Payne's gray.*

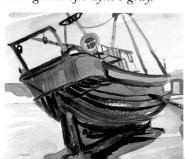

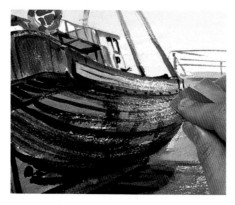

2 *Build up dark shadow tones on the hull with dry-brush. Tear off a small piece of medium grade sandpaper, and fold it. Rub it along the boat's hull, mostly on the side and a little on the back and lower part. Be careful not to rub off too much paint.*

3 *The combined textures of dry-brush on the beach, and dry-brush and sanded areas on the boat all work effectively in unison to capture the essence of this rugged subject.*

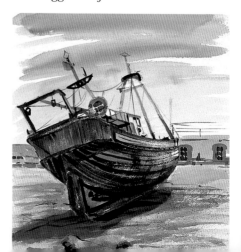

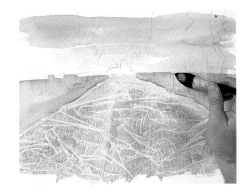

3 Fill in the rest of the picture with broad washes. Use ultramarine and violet in the sky, and burnt sienna and sap green on the ground. Leave to dry.

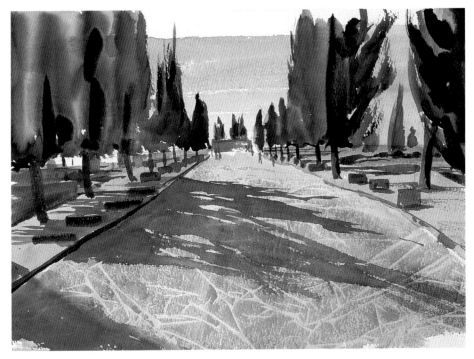

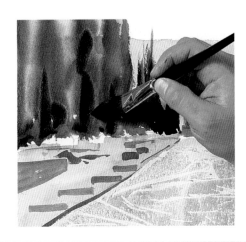

4 Paint the trees with a wash of burnt umber, brushing in vertical streaks of black while wet. Use burnt umber for the square blocks along the side of the road, burnt sienna through the trees on the left, and violet for the building at the road's end.

5 To complete the picture and bring it alive, paint the dynamic tree shadows with a mix of magenta and ultramarine. Glaze these over the road texture, uniting the composition.

VARIATION • 2
Imprinting with cardboard

1 *Lay an initial wash of cadmium yellow over all the picture, except the areas to be painted blue. Brush burnt umber onto the side of a piece of corrugated cardboard, and press it repeatedly onto the bridge. Repeat this on the foreground, using sap green on cardboard of a different texture. Apply some burnt umber washes over the tree trunks.*

2 *Use the card edges to create the branches of the tree on the left. Mix indigo and cerulean blue, and using a fresh piece of card, press some of this color above and below the bridge for foliage. Paint a cerulean blue wash on the distant mountains.*

3 *Use a fresh piece of torn card for each color and build up the colors around the picture. Finish off with cadmium orange on the foreground.*

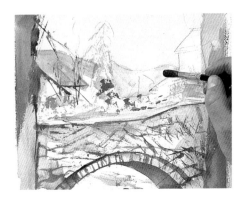

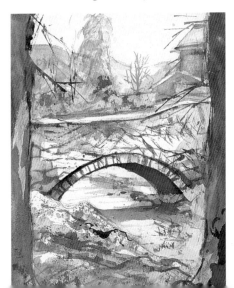

In context

Sometimes a textural technique such as scumbling may be used in a traditional watercolor to capture a specific effect. But some artists venture wholly into the world of textures and make such techniques a feature of their work almost to the point of abstraction. They inevitably develop their own personal repertoire of techniques, which may not be easily discerned by the onlooker.

A very dry scumble was applied here without too much pigment in order to create a fuzzy effect of fine barren trees. This was done using a medium hog's hair brush.

Snow Coppice
Mark Topham

The small amount of scumbling in this picture was used to portray the hazy winter shrubbery bare of leaves. The slightly grainy quality of the scumble created a nice contrast with the soft background and foreground gradated washes. Too much scumble would have altered the overall feeling.

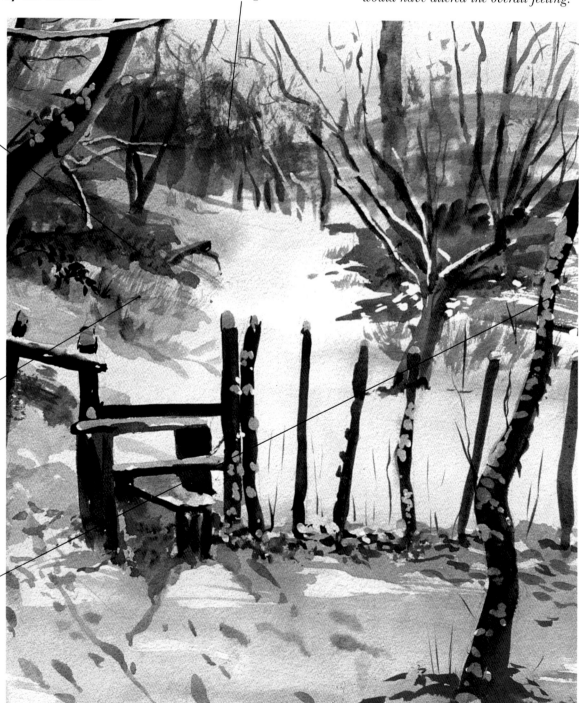

A dark, thick scumble was dabbed onto the dark green wash to give the impression of coarse vegetation.

This fairly wet scumble closely resembles a dry-brush technique. The strokes are all in one direction to represent blades of dry grass.

The clumps of snow on the upright tree trunk had to be masked with masking fluid before applying this medium-dry scumble. Care was needed to avoid scrubbing off the mask.

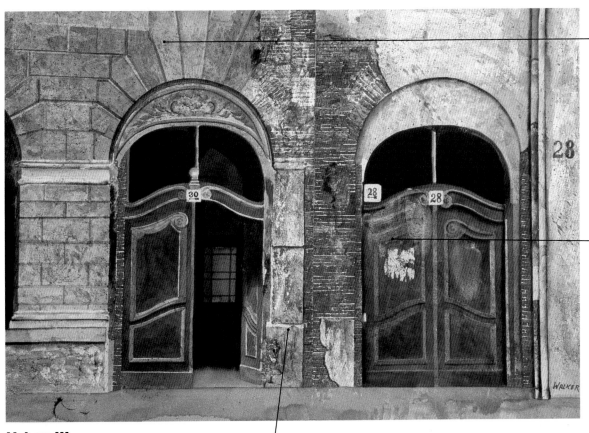

Pale gray washes support textural overpainting and plenty of spatter.

The original mottled brown texture of the door has been scratched and lifted off.

Urban III

Sandra Walker

This painting is all about texture. Each of the various kinds of surface have been treated with different textures, including the doors. At the same time the accurate recording of detail has served to give an almost photographic sense of realism.

These large stones have been treated with a coarse texture to suggest sandstone that has been weathered over the years.

There are many layers here, each produced in a different way. Methods used include masking, imprinting, wet-in-wet, and lifting off. The combined effect is complex and exciting.

This subdued part of the picture provides breathing space and is treated with subtle washes and gentle imprinted textures.

Sun Flowers

Benjamin Mall

The textures created here are intentionally abstract, designed to create a painting that is a play of texture and color. Numerous techniques developed by the artist have been used.

Yellow spatter has been sprayed on a dark blue area, as if cascading from the flowers. The freedom of the applied techniques belies the compositional skill needed to create a set of marks that work well together.

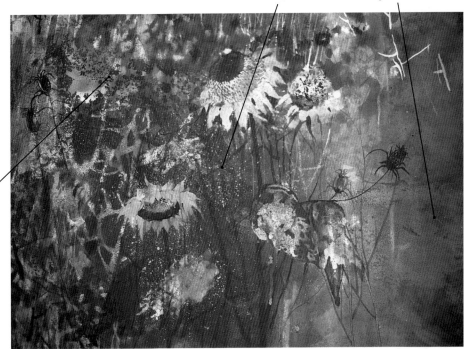

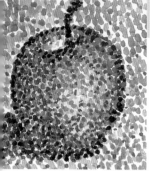

As shown by the Impressionists, the use of dots or flecks of color creates a scintillating effect. Rather than mixing colors on the palette, you apply them side by side so that they mix optically. Dots of different colors, interspersed in various proportions and viewed from a distance, fuse in an extraordinary way.

Decorator's brush

In this painting a coarse decorator's brush (in this case a 3 inch (7.5 cm), but a 2 or 1 inch (5 or 2.5 cm) would do), is chosen to make the hair-like marks that will represent the bundle of straggly vegetation. The wetness or dryness of the paint is crucial in determining the type of effect achieved.

Stippling

You can make small dots with the tip of a fine sable brush. The tip of a large, hog's hair or decorator's brush, which has a flat end, produces groups of tiny dots. Make the dots by dabbing with a downward, pecking motion, building up a mosaic of flecks. Continuous dabbing with different colors creates a flickering texture. A thick make-up brush splays nicely when wet, and makes medium-sized flecks. The best consistency for the paint is creamy, because if it is too wet the dots will merge, dissolve, or dry too faint.

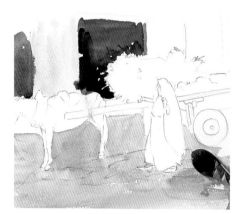

1 Paint the background buildings with flat washes of black, cerulean blue, and burnt umber, outlining the donkey and cart. Apply a wash of burnt sienna for the ground, painting around the donkey, woman, and cart. Use a mop brush that can be drawn to a point or a smaller sable.

2 Paint the donkey and cart in burnt umber using a No. 9 round sable. Paint the vegetation in sap green with a little black in places, dropping more concentrated paint into the wet surface later. Paint the woman's clothes in pale indigo, immediately adding concentrated streaks into the wet paint.

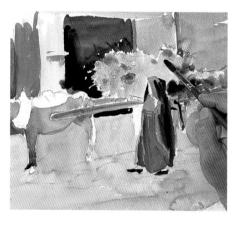

VARIATION • 1
Stipple build-up

1 *Lay initial pale washes of Hooker's green and burnt umber. Mix cadmium red with yellow and stipple on with the same brush while parts of the washes are still damp. Use a dryer mix as well, allowing the hairs to separate and splay slightly.*

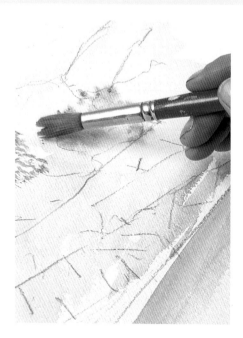

2 *Apply burnt sienna to damp and dry areas, using the same stippling technique. Create flecks of different shapes and sizes by varying the pressure on the brush.*

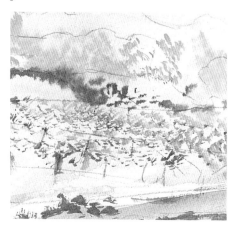

3 Build up the donkey using black and burnt umber. Use a mix of burnt umber and burnt sienna to paint the shaded ground, including the shadow cast by the donkey. With the decorator's brush, stipple a fairly wet solution onto the ground to represent the texture of sand and earth.

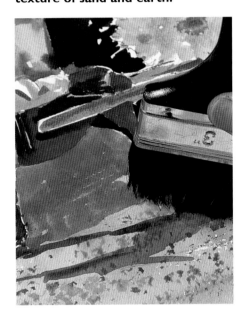

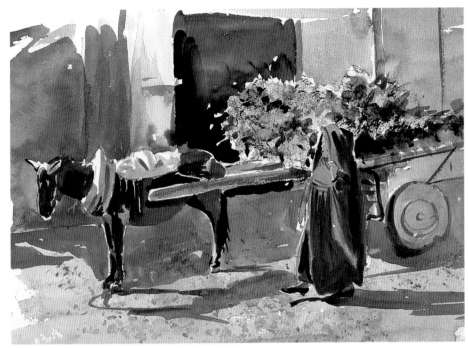

4 Use the decorator's brush to stipple a fairly wet solution of viridian on the vegetation. When dry, follow with a thick, almost dry mix of sap green and black. This second layer will have a finer, hairier texture.

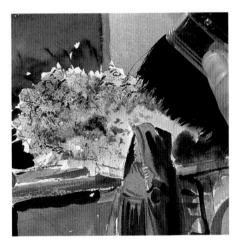

5 Complete the painting by adding a little more detail, as needed, to the donkey, cart, and woman. Add a few brushstrokes in sap green and black to the vegetation to suggest shaded areas.

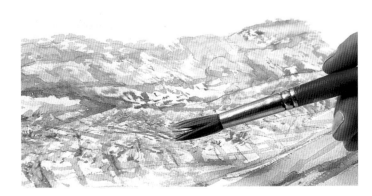

3 *Build up the stipple with consecutive layers of ultramarine, violet, cadmium yellow, and Hooker's green. Paint some long strokes of ultramarine to represent tree trunks and their shadows.*

4 *Build up the foliage with further layers of Hooker's green and cadmium red. Use sepia to emphasize the tree trunks and to suggest branches. These few brushstrokes prevent this painting from becoming almost completely abstract.*

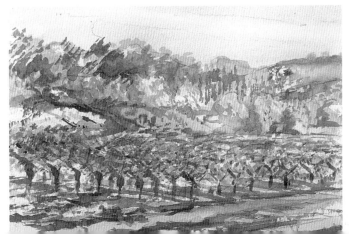

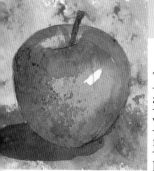

The sponge is a wonderfully versatile supplement to the brush, producing quite a different effect. It provides a "hands on" way of generating naturally convoluted textures that you dab on to build up foliage or weathered effects on rocks. By dragging the sponge you can create a streaked effect, similar to grass or bare branches.

Sponge painting

Sponges vary enormously, so keep a few different types, natural and synthetic, fine and coarse. After mixing a pool of paint – either creamy or very runny depending on the effect you want – soak it up with the sponge. A sponge will hold a lot of paint, and you can exploit this, squeezing the paint onto the surface for a very wet effect, or applying it with light pressure for a delicate effect. You can use a large sponge to damp down a large surface area, and apply a wash with it on a wet or dry surface. Thick paint in a sponge will create dry-sponge effects. To clean a sponge, submerge it in water and squeeze out all the paint. Repeat, if necessary.

Directional strokes

You can use a sponge in a similar way to a brush by stroking or dragging it to elongate the paint texture, in imitation of the foliage of certain trees. Tear off a piece of sponge to create a rough surface to work with. Keep a fine sponge for finer textures.

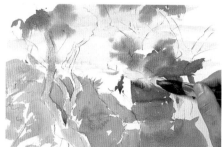

1 First paint the sea with a pale wash of cerulean blue. For the trees, drop in some burnt umber, and then some olive green into the umber, making the paint wetter for the more distant leaves. Work in burnt sienna and paint the foreground with wet-on-dry washes.

2 When dry, use a coarse sponge to apply dilute olive green to the distant trees. Drag the sponge a little in different directions to vary the direction of the texture.

VARIATION • 1
Sponge build-up

1 *Lay down an initial variegated wash of burnt sienna, burnt umber, and yellow ocher for the trees, house, and ground, cobalt blue for the sky, and ultramarine for the shadows on the house. When it is dry, dab a thicker consistency of burnt sienna over the leaf area with a fine sponge.*

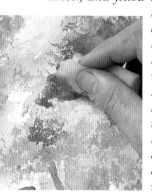

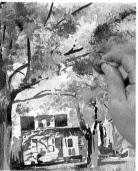

2 *While the burnt sienna is still damp, paint in some branches with black and burnt umber. Paint the details on the house in black. Next, sponge burnt sienna and olive green over the ground. When the leaves are dry, go over them with a mix of concentrated burnt sienna and a little black.*

3 *Sponging has been used for the largest proportion of this painting with only supplementary brushwork on the house and tree. Varying the thickness of the sponging gives the painting vitality.*

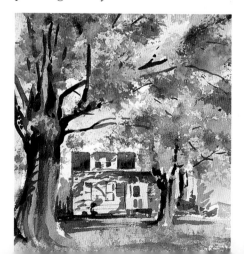

3 This close-up shows the effect of flicking the sponge at different angles to represent the spiky foliage of an olive tree.

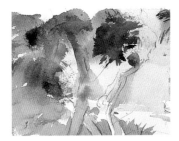

4 Continue the same technique with the trees on the other side of the path. Vary the effect by rolling the sponge on its side. Use different sides of the sponge for different textures.

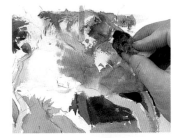

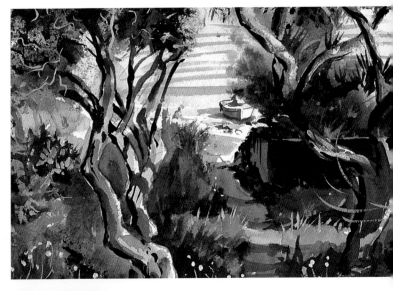

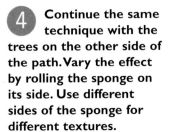

5 Using a brush, paint the details of the scene in ultramarine, Hooker's green dark, burnt sienna, burnt umber, yellow ocher, and black. Take a very fine sponge and dab a fine texture of black over the existing paint for the leaves in deep shade.

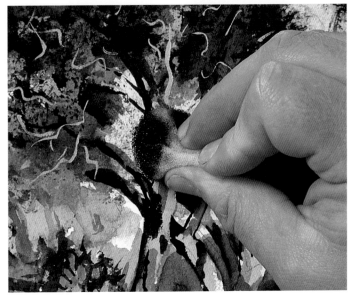

6 The sponge painting technique has been confined to the top foliage. It does not dominate or overwhelm but has been integrated into the overall composition, adding another dimension to the picture, and adding an exciting realism to the trees.

VARIATION • 2
Assorted sponge marks

1 *Apply initial, small, wet-in-wet washes with a natural sponge. Then apply a second layer of color, stippling with and dragging the sponge over the paper in long, dry streaks.*

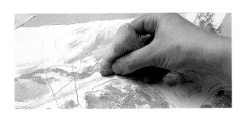

2 *This close-up of a rock shows the complexity of color mixtures that you can build up by repeated stippling with a sponge.*

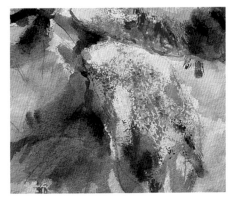

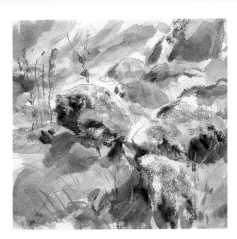

3 *The finished painting, with the exception of a few details, has almost entirely been done with a sponge, showing how versatile a tool this is.*

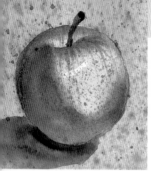

Spattering

Spattering is an exciting and popular medium with special qualities, not least of which is the ease with which you can produce an impressive effect. A fine spray gives a realistic interpretation of sand and stones, whilst large splashes impart vivacity and excitement in expressive style. Spattering is best used as a supplement to regular painting.

A toothbrush is the most popular tool for spraying paint. The amount of control possible depends on how close the surface is. To protect areas from spray, use pieces of paper as a mask. Dot size will vary depending on the quantity of paint in the brush. For large, splashed dots, tap a paintbrush onto a finger, about 6 inches (15cm) from the surface. Do this carefully because, as the hairs rebound, liquid flies in the opposite direction. A diffuser will project a medium and fine spray over a wide area and needs plenty of paint mixed in a jar. Water spattered into a wet wash displaces paint in puddles. For reverse dots, spray masking fluid onto a dry surface, then paint.

Spatter and masking fluid

In this painting, the sun has bleached out the visible texture on the ground, therefore the spatter is visible only in the shadows. These shadows have complicated shapes so using masking fluid is the best way to capture them. You can mask the surrounding areas by taping on sheets of paper, thus confining the spattered paint to the areas you want.

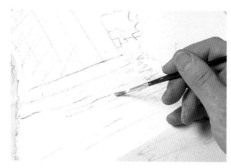

1 Lay a pale wash of cadmium red on the forecourt and sap green on the surrounding foliage. With a No. 2 brush, paint masking fluid over the sunlit areas on the forecourt and over the sunny spots on the bushes. Leave to dry.

2 Paint washes of cadmium yellow, sap green, Prussian blue, and black on the bushes. Allow them to mix on the paper surface. Paint indigo on the garage door, leaving a little white paper showing, and ultramarine on the garage walls.

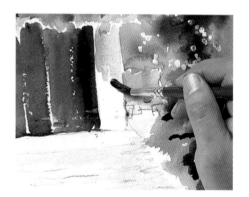

VARIATION · I
Spattering body color

I *Paint the sky wet-in-wet with intense concentrations of Antwerp blue and Payne's gray. Keep the sea spray area clear of paint by dabbing with tissue. When the sky is dry, dry-brush the sea with Payne's gray. Paint the rocks in a mix of black and sepia, and the distant land in Payne's gray.*

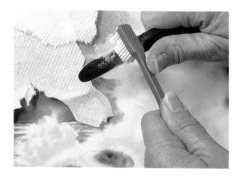

2 *Mask everything except the sea spray area. Load white gouache onto a toothbrush and spray it on by dragging a knife blade backwards across the bristles.*

3 *This is a simple but dramatically beautiful painting. The fine spray creates an ethereal glow set against the dramatic sky. The dry-brushed sea also adds to the overall effect of a scene bathed in moonlight.*

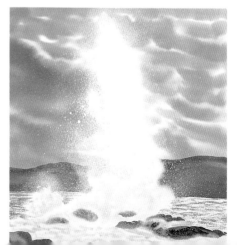

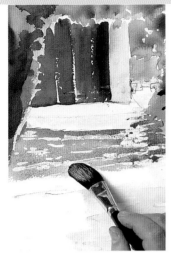

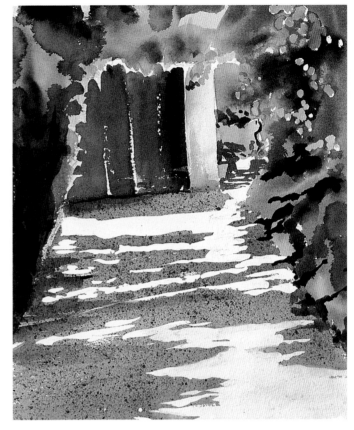

4 Tape sheets of paper around the sides of the forecourt. Using a toothbrush, spatter on layers of burnt sienna and Payne's gray. Have kitchen paper ready to dab away any overlarge dots or any excessive concentrations of spattered dots.

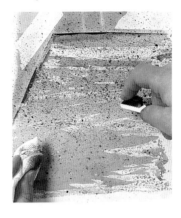

3 Apply washes: violet at the garage end, then burnt sienna, and Payne's gray in the foreground. Remove masking fluid from the bushes and then paint flowers in cadmium red and yellow.

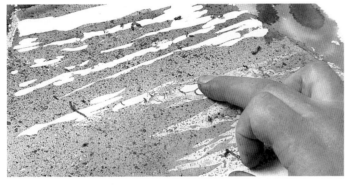

5 Remove the paper masks. Make sure that the spattered paint is completely dry before you start to rub off the masking fluid.

6 Add a little Payne's gray in the left-hand part of the shadow, immediately under the bushes, to intensify it. The forecourt shadows are hard-edged, conveying the intensity of the sunlight overhead.

VARIATION · 2
Spatter with paintbrush

1 *Paint the background in indigo and magenta, and the foreground with sap green, burnt umber, yellow ocher, burnt sienna, and a little ultramarine. Use a paintbrush for spattering the woodland path, but don't overload it. Tap it sharply on your finger or a ruler.*

2 *A brush is harder to control than a toothbrush, so add a fine spray over a wider area with the toothbrush.*

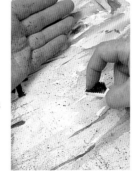

3 *When the spattering is finished, paint the long foreground shadows in single brushstrokes.*

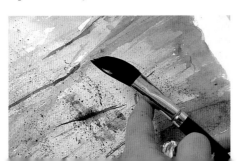

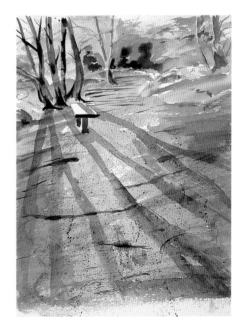

In context

Stipple and sponge-painting are used in the paintings on these pages in distinctive and individual ways. These techniques are very important to watercolor and each has a wide scope and can be adapted to vastly different circumstances, depending on the subject and the effect the artist requires. In these paintings these techniques have been subtly incorporated into the composition.

Winter in the City

Janis Theodore

This unusual painting has great stillness. The falling snow has been sprayed on using a toothbrush and white body color. The paint has been carefully controlled, with the size of dots slightly increased in the foreground, even subjecting the snow to the laws of perspective.

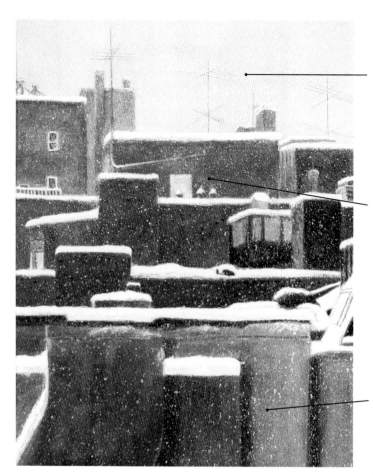

Due to the paleness of the overcast sky only the larger dots are clearly visible. Some extra dots have been added with a fine-pointed brush.

The distant buildings are paler, due to the weather conditions. The spray is finer, just as the snowflakes would seem smaller from a distance.

The foreground spray is coarser and has a downward directional force to the dots, giving an impression of falling snow.

Margaret's July

Carol Ann Schrader

This artist uses stipple as a form of detailing. The very fine dots can be seen only by close inspection. This is a slow process that can produce exquisite results. By using tiny dots you can intermingle different colors, which will optically mix in a similar way to that achieved by the printing process.

With the exception of the veins, the whole leaf is built up with a collection of very fine dots of different shades of green, producing a lovely mottled texture.

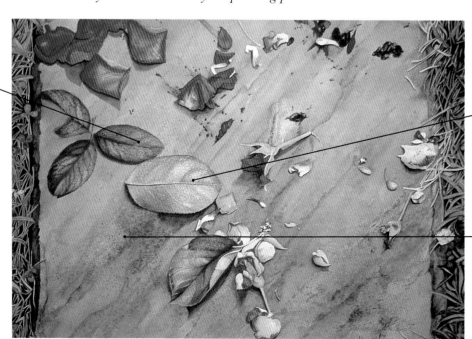

White body color has been stippled on for the highlighted raised parts of the leaf, while a bluish green has been used for the rest of the leaf. Stipple is a very effective way to show rounded form with varying areas of tone.

This is a much coarser stipple than is used on the leaves, and is well-suited to the algae and rough texture of the stone. The individual hairs of the bristle brush that was used are in evidence.

Evening, Williamson Park, Lancaster

Maurice Read

The sponge is frequently used to portray vegetation and trees, as in this atmospheric painting. The natural impressions left by a sponge mimic the appearance of foliage. The overall effect is soft and is consistent with the treatment of the rest of the painting.

A sponge was used to apply some sepia to the dome to give an aged look. It was applied rather wet, to allow it to fuse and blend a little, assisted by some brushwork.

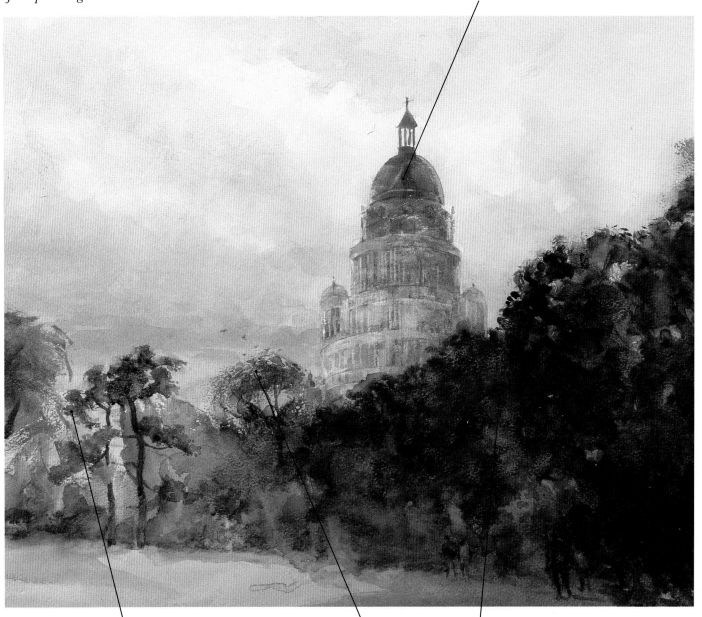

The foliage of these trees was built up with a fine sponge, with a more stippled effect around the edges.

The fine grain made by the sponge has been enhanced with brushwork to bulk it out, and cause some of the grain to merge.

The main body of trees has been built up with wet-in-wet washes applied fairly concentrated and overlaid with sponge-painting to give texture.

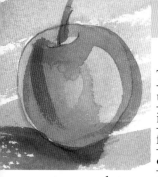

This technique is useful for sketching because it is fast and expressive, or it can be added to complete a painting. Above all, though, it is an extremely fresh and spontaneous way of working. You can use brush drawing effectively in conjunction with washes. The brush produces modulated and energetic lines which are good for portraying movement.

Using a rigger

This painting consists of two basic ingredients: flat washes applied with a mop brush, which can be drawn to a point to circumscribe the shapes accurately; and linear detail, achieved with a size 1 sable rigger, which was ideal for describing the many folds and creases of the evening dress.

Brush drawing

A flexible, pointed brush is the most suitable for this technique, sable being preferable because it combines the correct degree of softness, firmness, and flexibility so that when you lift it off the paper it springs back into shape. For brush drawing, you will need to be able to draw and to keep a flexible wrist. Balance the brush in your hand, midway along the stem, and hold it loosely. As you draw a line, press downward on the paper to spread the hairs out and widen the line. A fairly concentrated but fluid mixture of paint and water is best for solid lines, and you can achieve an interesting variation using the dry-brush technique.

1 Use the mop brush to paint a mix of violet and a touch of Payne's gray over the background in energetic diagonal strokes that allow the paper to break up the paint. Paint around the outline of the figure, without too much concern for meticulous accuracy as a little overlapping is acceptable.

2 Using the same mop brush, block in the dress with diluted black. Suggest the skin and hair with mixes of Naples yellow, Venetian red, and burnt umber. Use the rigger to paint the shapes and folds in the dress with indigo. Vary the thickness of the lines, letting them curve and break up at the end of the strokes.

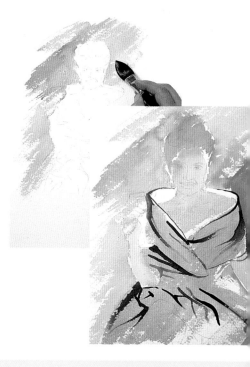

VARIATION • 1
Using a large brush

1 *Use a 4B graphite stick on a medium grain paper for the under drawing. The swirling movement of the subject is quickly established with a few bold sweeps.*

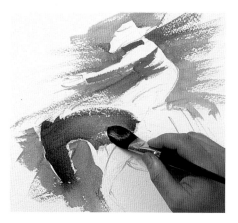

2 *Paint the background in strokes away from the torso with burnt umber and Venetian red. Do this with sideways flicks of the brush. Use Prussian blue under the horse and brown madder alizarin for its head and neck.*

3 *Paint the horse's body, the saddle, and the man's legs in a few quick strokes, all of which break up at the end of the stroke. The grain of the paper helps to portray the sense of movement. Use a smaller brush to apply burnt umber for the man's hat.*

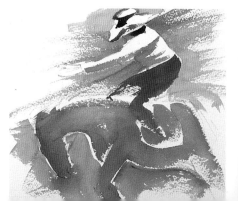

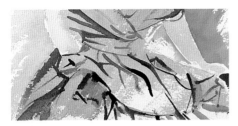

3 The line work gives the dress definition and suggests the qualities of the satin material. Indicate shadows with a few small washes of indigo, which also help to balance out the line work.

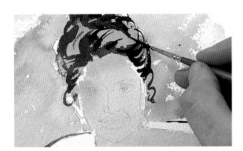

4 Use expressive line work to paint the wavy hair in burnt umber and black. Follow this by carefully painting in the features, using a minimum of brushmarks.

5 Paint the glass simply using indigo on the glass handle and burnt umber with black for the liquid. Too much detail here would overemphasize a secondary part of the composition.

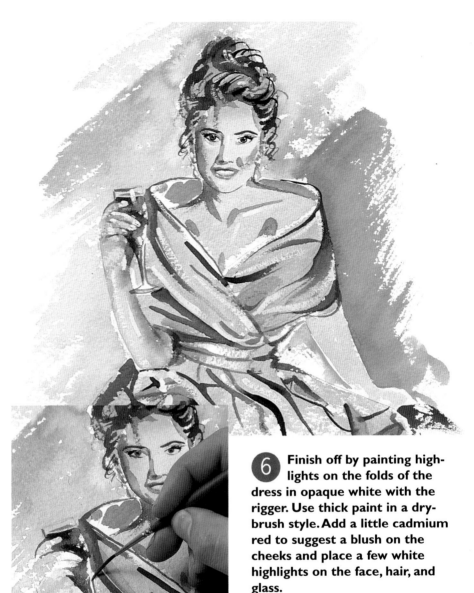

6 Finish off by painting highlights on the folds of the dress in opaque white with the rigger. Use thick paint in a dry-brush style. Add a little cadmium red to suggest a blush on the cheeks and place a few white highlights on the face, hair, and glass.

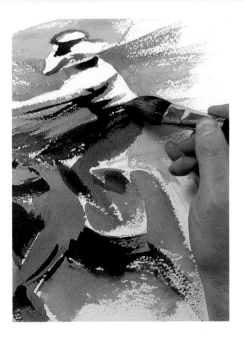

4 *Using indigo with a little black, paint the horse's mane and body detail and the shaded side of the man's body. Continue using a minimum of quick brushstrokes; a blurred sense of speed is the main objective.*

5 *The explosion of unharnessed energy in this scene is captured by the use of strong directional brushstrokes. The brushwork is free and uncluttered with only a suggestion of individual shapes. Every element has been given a sense of movement and the cumulative effect is dynamic.*

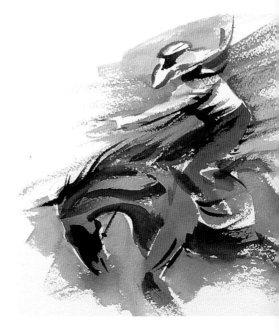

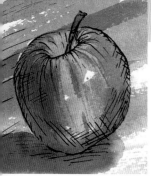

This is a happy marriage of two techniques. The line takes on a descriptive role and becomes the binding factor, freeing the wash to extend beyond its normal boundaries without the need for hard edges, and allowing the wet-in-wet properties to be exploited fully. Line and wash is particularly popular with illustrators.

Line and wash

The line can be in pencil, ink or paint, and applied with dip pen, fountain pen, or brush. Hot-pressed paper (see Before You Start, page 10) is the easiest surface for line work because of its smoothness, but cold-pressed papers produce more variety. Generally, washes should be pale to give the line greater emphasis. Black lines should not be too heavy but delicate and refined; sepia or brown lines are more subtle. For variable thickness of line, the dip pen, with its flexible nib, is ideal. There are no rules regarding the sequence of work. You can draw the lines first, followed by a wash, or vice-versa (in which case an initial pencil drawing is necessary).

Using water soluble ink

A crisp initial line drawing is formed by using water-soluble ink and a dip pen. Dampening some areas allows the ink to spread a little. Subsequent washes of paint will further dissolve and soften the lines of the drawing.

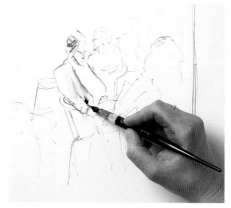

1 Use a fine-grained hot-pressed paper or illustration board. Place a little water where you want soft lines to appear. Use the flexibility of the nib to create an interesting variety of line by varying the pressure as you draw.

2 Using a No. 4 round sable, brush over part of the line with clean water, causing it to dissolve and run. This will create a softer line and an associated pale wash.

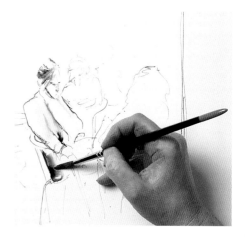

VARIATION • 1
Waterproof ink

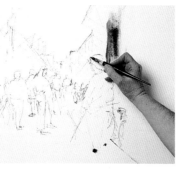

1 *Use a medium-grained cold-pressed watercolor paper in order to incorporate some dry-brush at a later stage. Do the initial drawing in Indian ink using a dip pen, with the knowledge that once dry the waterproof ink will not dissolve with subsequent washes.*

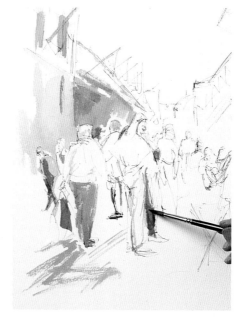

2 *Apply loose washes in selective areas, with a No. 4 round sable. Use diluted ink or a pale wash of black watercolor. Do not strictly adhere to the lines, but leave patches of white paper showing. Take advantage of the rough surface texture to do some dry brushwork.*

3 Apply a pale wash of raw sienna to the hair and a mix of rose madder and raw sienna for the skin tones. Use loose brush-strokes that partially dissolve the line work. Be sure to leave some white paper showing through.

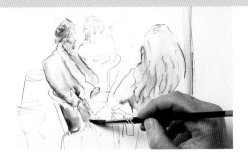

5 This close up shows how subtle colors, interspersed with white paper, give an airy feeling of light permeating the café. Much movement and atmosphere is also conveyed by the expressive line work.

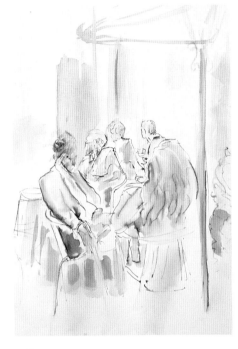

4 Complete the painting with washes of viridian and cobalt blue over the background and figures. Leave some of the line work unpainted over so that it remains crisp and sharp.

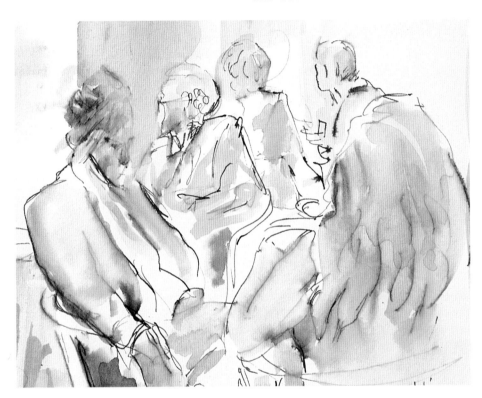

3 *With the broader washes in place, use pen and ink to add some darker lines and detail, especially to the foreground figure, giving it prominence. Use dark brushstrokes to accentuate the perspective of the street with some diagonal lines converging on the center.*

4 *Finally go over the picture with two pale washes – cerulean blue around the street level and yellow ocher in the sky and foreground. This final touch of color helps to give the picture depth.*

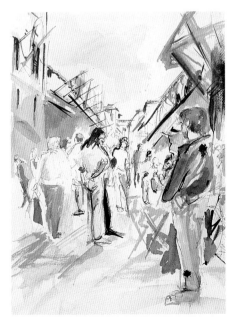

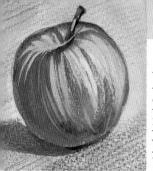

Watercolor is compatible with many other media which, when combined, mutually enhance one another. For example, the striking brilliance and grainy texture of soft pastel contrasts with the smoothness of watercolor, while a subtle watercolor wash adds body and atmosphere to a color pencil sketch without completely dominating the picture.

Mixed media

When combining soft pastels with watercolor, paint the watercolor first to establish the background, then apply the pastels on top. If you worked the other way, you would lose the pastel texture. Pastels work particularly well on grainy watercolor paper, biting into the fiber, and forming a rough texture that can be smoothed with a finger, rag, or brush. Colored pencils can be combined with watercolor in any order. If you brush water over soluble pencils they will partially dissolve, farther harmonizing with watercolor, but they will need rubbing to dissipate completely. The advantage of including pencils in this technique is the vigorous sketchy lines and hatching that can complement watercolor painting. When mixing two media, they should not appear separate but in harmony: their contrasting differences are their strength.

Watercolor and oil pastels

The intense colors and rich luster of oil pastels complement the delicacy of watercolor. They can be used in any order. If the oil pastel is put down first, it will have a resist effect similar to that of wax crayons. The combination also works well if you first paint the washes and work over the top with the pastels.

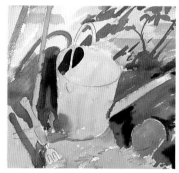

1 Build up the picture with watercolor washes of Indian red and burnt sienna for the wall, and Payne's gray, violet, Prussian blue, and Hooker's green for the remaining areas.

2 Using a Hooker's green oil pastel, give the plants a little definition. This produces a coarse textured line, so you won't be aiming for fine detail but a textured rendering. Use an Indian red oil pastel in the flowerpot.

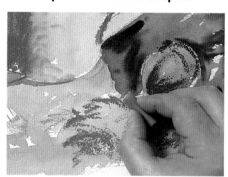

VARIATION • 1
Watercolor and color pencils

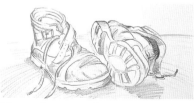

1 *Using a hot-pressed watercolor paper for its finer grain, do your initial drawing with waterproof colored pencils. Capture the character of the boots and the texture of the leather with hatching and loose line work.*

2 *Lay washes of violet, burnt umber, and Payne's gray over the background and foreground. Then freely apply washes of burnt sienna, yellow ocher, violet, and Payne's gray over the boots. Leave white paper for the highlights.*

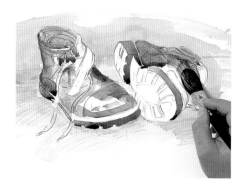

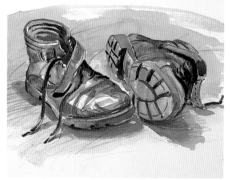

3 *Apply further washes to the darker areas, using more concentrated color. Work over the boots again in colored pencil to reinforce the underdrawing, adding detail for the laces, the buckle, and the straps.*

3 Use the side of a piece of burnt sienna pastel to color the wall. This produces a perfect rendition of coarse brickwork. Use violet, ultramarine, and Payne's gray pastel on the watering can.

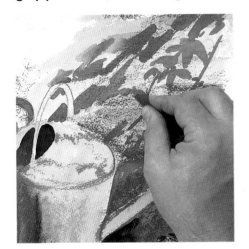

4 Use a black pastel to add definition and darken the shadows. This color is very concentrated and shouldn't be overused.

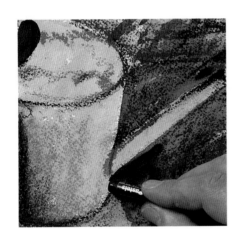

5 Use white oil pastel to draw attention to features otherwise lost, such as the rim of the watering can base. Highlight the handles on the fork and rake. Add white texture to the brighter parts of the watering can.

6 The finished picture shows how the two media work together to give depth and texture. Both mediums use the paper in a completely different way, the watercolor benefitting from the high absorption of the paper to produce an even flat wash, while the pastel benefits from its rough surface texture.

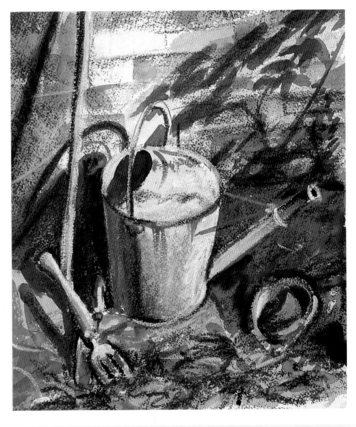

VARIATION • 2
Watercolor and soft pastel

1 *Lay a flat wash of ultramarine over the whole picture except the fire. With a No. 7 brush, work indigo into the wet paint for the darkest shadows. Paint the flames in cadmium red and yellow. Paint sepia washes over the darkest shadows and to define the details.*

2 *When the paint is thoroughly dry, use cadmium red and yellow soft pastels to suggest the reflections of the flames around the room. Use emerald green, ultramarine, and burnt umber in the carpet and shadows. Apply the pastels with light, feathery strokes in a textural fashion.*

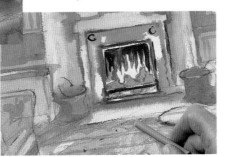

3 *The grainy pastels suggest the flickering light, and so perfectly capture the atmosphere of the room.*

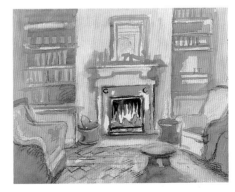

In context

These three paintings show mixed media, brush-drawing and line and wash used in a variety of circumstances and styles. Seeing these techniques used in a range of different contexts can help to expand understanding of the potential of each.

Sunlight on Trees

Maurice Read

Watercolor, body color, and color pencils were used in this woodland scene. The watercolor was first laid in blue-gray washes with a limited palette. These provide the underlying tonal structure. The color pencils and body color were applied over this to provide the splashes of vivid color.

Watercolor was used for the pale background washes. The tree trunks were silhouetted with darker washes.

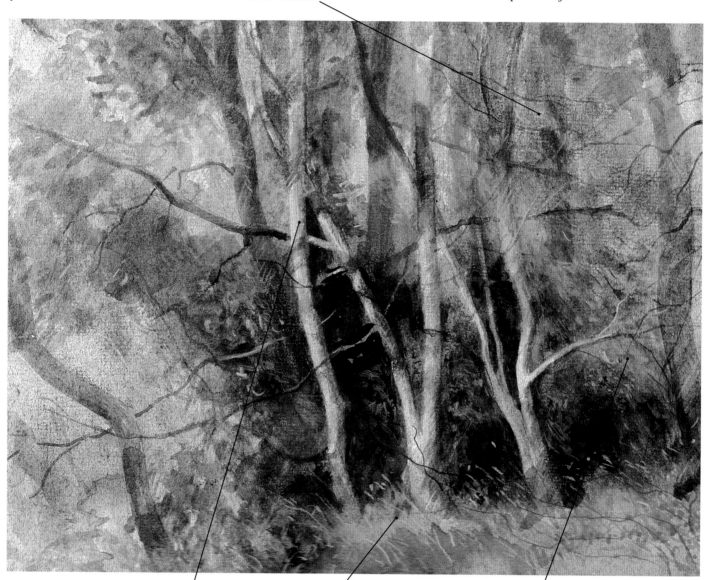

The tree trunks were blocked in with yellow color pencil, broken at intervals by areas of shadow.

Individual streaks and dashes were made with several different color pencils, to suggest grass.

Small flecks of body color were scumbled between the tree trunks to suggest undergrowth.

Arles
E Gordon West

This painting contains very linear brush-drawing and washes are used to fill in the forms in a similar way to a line-and-wash technique. This work doesn't contain any of the sweeping strokes usually associated with brush-drawing, but it has a subdued character of its own.

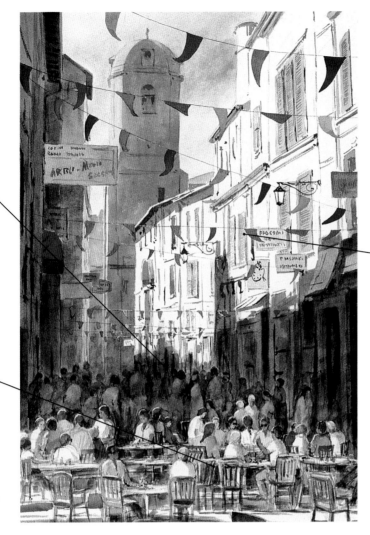

The figures in the crowd are drawn simply. Much of the linework is blended and absorbed into the dark wash. There is just enough information to suggest the crowd and keep it interesting.

A lot of careful linework is used to draw the chairs. Their angles and positions are very accurate, clearly letting the sun break through from the left. The inclusion of the tops of the three foreground chairs helps to give the correct feeling of distance.

Apart from simple washes on the shutters, these buildings are entirely treated with simple linework that clearly shows the linear perspective. Much of the paper here is left white.

Line is used in a textural way here by loosely scribbling and hatching across the surface. The washes are simple and flat.

The detail is shared between the washes and linework. Small washes describe most of the detail, with loose lines used to provide consistency.

Cornish Village
Tom Groom

This picture shows a traditional use of line and wash. The pen and ink line is strong and textural as a result of the use of a medium-textured watercolor paper. The washes are clean and simple, and use a limited palette of earthy colors. White paper has been left for the white buildings.

The center of interest is indicated by the strongest color, a reddish brown. The linework is loose and expressive to convey a sense of movement as the figures walk down the hill.

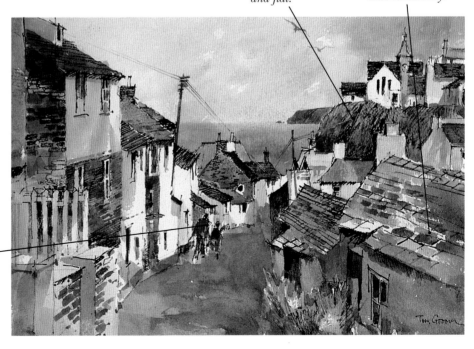

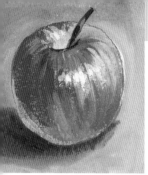

"Translucent" is perhaps the most accurate way to describe water-color as there is a range of pigments, from very transparent to opaque. Chinese white, for example, sits at the opaque end of the spectrum. Opaque water-based paint such as gouache can be used alongside watercolors, adding extra qualities without spoiling the overall luminosity. Observe the difference when the paint is dry. Opaque paint sits on the surface, while a transparent wash recedes, giving a feeling of space.

Opaque highlights

The initial deep-toned background washes are freely laid down in the knowledge that lighter colors can easily be added later, so delaying those decisions until the final stages, when an overall assessment is easier to make. As a result, a few selective highlights can be added without diminishing the effect of the deep shadows.

Body color

Chinese white mixed with other colors in concentrated form produces more covering power; when it is more diluted, it simply modifies colors into paler and more pastel hues, an effect that is very pleasant and is worth exploring. A more concentrated white is offered by gouache. This is more brilliant but more chalky, and is better if you want to achieve a thick consistency. You can extend into the full range of gouache paints, working opaquely over washes, which will enable you to work from dark to light. If you include gum arabic with gouache, you can build up rich, translucent glazes.

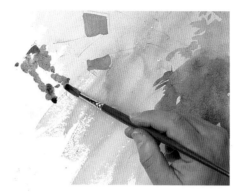

1 The main part of the background wash is made up of ultramarine and alizarin violet, with a little burnt sienna down one side. When dry, apply washes representing foliage in mixtures of yellow ocher, sap green, and ultramarine on the right-hand side, and a little burnt umber on the left.

2 Block in the large banana leaves with a mix of ultramarine and yellow ocher, and extend down into the creepers using a darker version of the same color. Paint the dark leaves in the center in indigo. When dry, overpaint the cast shadows of the banana leaves.

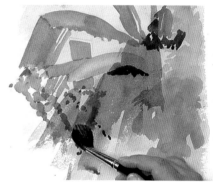

VARIATION • I
Pastel skin tones

I Make a preliminary drawing using a 3B pencil on a medium-grained paper. Then paint burnt sienna and cerulean blue separately around the head and on the shoulders. Apply a thin wash of raw sienna loosely to the face, followed by burnt sienna. Brush a darker mix into the hair, eyebrows, and mustache.

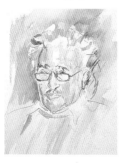

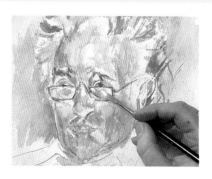

2 Apply raw sienna to the face, burnt sienna and phthalo blue into the hair, and to emphasize the features. For stronger tones, paint areas of cadmium red over the burnt sienna. Add small touches of Chinese white and cadmium red mix. Apply Chinese white thickly for highlights on the spectacles, and face, and also on the hair.

3 Intensify the background with dark washes of viridian and raw sienna. The coolness of this wash frames the warm face colors, causing the face to come forward in a three-dimensional way. To finish, dab and stroke Chinese white with a minute touch of viridian onto the face and hair.

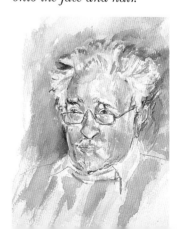

3 Note how the shadows of the overlaid blue banana leaf have partially dissolved the dark creepers causing pleasant softening. The darkest areas of the foliage, painted in indigo, are situated in the bottom right, counterbalancing the bright top section. The darkest tones are mainly complete.

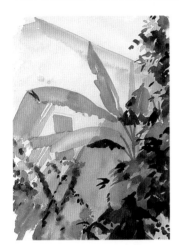

4 Mix a little permanent white gouache with cadmium yellow and a small amount of water using a No. 4 sable. Paint onto the upright central banana leaf. Add sap green to the mix and apply highlights to the pale foliage. Paint highlights on the banana leaves with white and a touch of yellow.

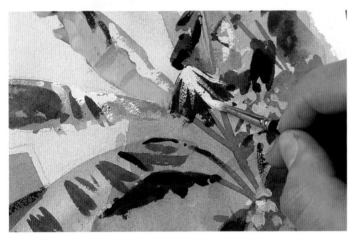

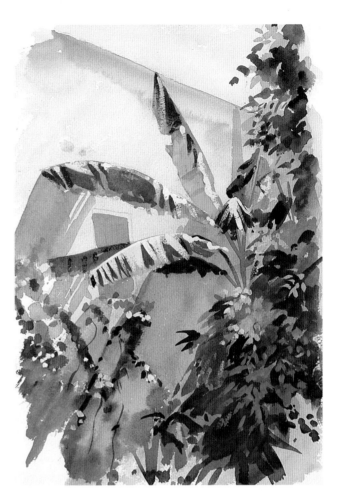

5 The final result is full of exciting contrasts, with a few carefully placed highlights over the diagonal shadows to convey the strong overhead sunlight. The low viewing angle suggests that the viewer is also in the shade. The triangular composition and strong diagonals give a dynamic feeling with a sense of life and warmth.

VARIATION • 2
Gouache and watercolor

1 *Outline the separate color areas in pencil. Then apply a wash wet-on-dry to the background, loosely suggesting foliage, using viridian, sap green, burnt umber, and black. Allow these colors to intermingle. When dry, paint black and Prussian blue gouache densely on the main body with a No. 10 brush.*

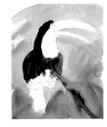

2 *Apply cadmium yellow, with a touch of burnt umber to the toucan's chest. Paint sap green, cadmium yellow, and cadmium red thickly on the top beak and eye area, and sap green with Prussian blue along the bottom beak. Dab cadmium red and cadmium yellow mixes thickly onto the chest.*

3 *Use Prussian blue for the feet. Then paint a thick mix of black and burnt umber on the branch. Finish with thick cadmium yellow. Paint thin black lines to separate the beak from the head, and in the eye and ribbing on the feet. Finally mix white and yellow and dab on the chest, beak, and eye.*

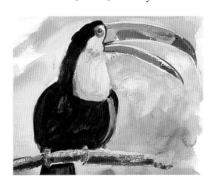

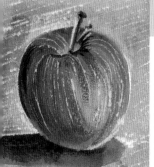

Considering the delicacy and finesse of water-color painting, it is a surprise to discover how tough watercolor paper is and how much punishment it can take. When you scrape back, you will alter the surface texture, but even this can be turned to your advantage as a roughened paper surface is very textural—so don't be afraid to get rough!

Scraping back

You may have to make important decisions as you come to the end of a painting and discover mistakes. To correct errors or alter an area so that it works better, you can scrape off the paint and possibly the top layer of paper as well. A scalpel point will scratch out fine lines or small areas. If you want a crisp edge, lightly cut into the paper over the outline: this is safest with heavy paper. A curved scalpel blade makes wider lines and a razor blade is good for large areas, but double-tape over one edge for safety. Scraping back works best on a dry surface because a damp surface will "fur up." Don't try to cut too deep with the first stroke, rather do several light strokes; in this way, you will cause minimum damage. Blunt blades will tear the paper.

Curved scalpel blade

A curved blade has the benefits of both a fine point for scraping out detail and a curved edge to scoop out broader areas. This painting needs scalpel blade techniques, as fine lines appear around the clock face and texture is needed on the wall and glass vase.

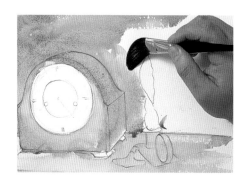

2 Reinforce the front of the clock body with two coats of burnt umber, applying some concentrated downward streaks in the second coat for wood grain. Use burnt sienna for a second layer on the side of the clock. Build up the wall texture and clock shadow with brown madder alizarin.

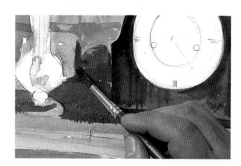

1 Use a mop brush to paint the wall and clock body in burnt sienna mixed with a little brown madder alizarin. Make large sweeping strokes, allowing the paper texture to show in some areas. Paint the tiled mantelpiece, candle, and vase with yellow ocher.

VARIATION • 1
Fine lines

1 *Paint the back- and foreground with a variegated wash of viridian, Payne's gray, and raw sienna, reserving the area for the kitten and flowers. Go over the top section with a strong mix of viridian, burnt sienna, and black.*

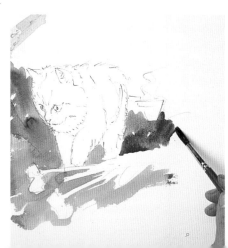

2 *Use a No. 3 sable to paint the cat's fur in combinations of violet and burnt sienna. To suggest fur, leave soft edges around the cat, particularly where it meets the dark area above.*

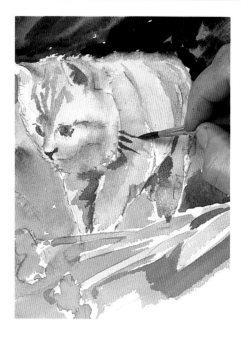

3 Build up detail of the wheat in the vase, the candle, clock, and clock key. Use Payne's gray for the clock face. When dry, take a scalpel with a curved blade and use the curved edge to scrape out highlights on the clock face. Use the point to scribe around the rim.

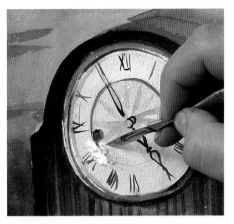

5 In the same way define highlights on the ears of wheat, the wall, and the tiles. Use the point of the blade to scrape fine lines on the brass candleholder and key.

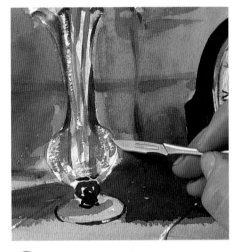

4 Scrape around the bowl of the vase with the curved edge of the blade, gouging out beads of white paper to represent the sparkling crystal reflections. Use the same technique for the neck of the vase.

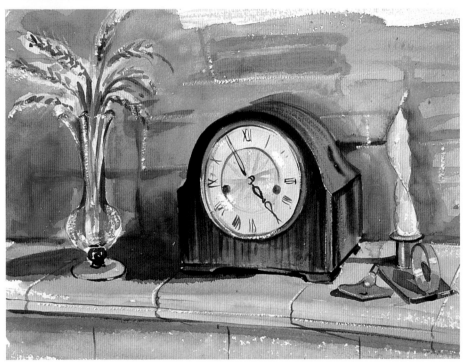

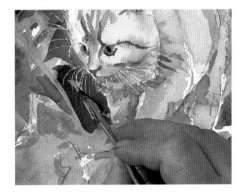

3 *Complete the detail of the cat's face and of the foliage and flowers. Allow to dry. Use a pointed scalpel blade and, with careful control, scratch clean curved lines outward from the cat's face to suggest whiskers.*

4 *The scratched out whiskers – the only place in this painting where this technique is used – provide sharp contrast to the remaining mainly wet-in-wet picture. This gives greater prominence to the cat's face and draws attention to the intense concentration in its eyes.*

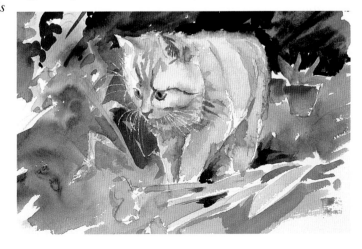

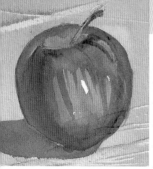

This is a good, clean way to create the illusion of blades of grass, branches or hair in wet paint, in a convincing and spontaneous way. It's an effect hard to reproduce with a brush and has a pleasantly textured edge, resulting in natural cohesion with its surroundings.

Paint brush handle

Most brush handles have a point, providing a convenient instrument for scouring impressions on the paper surface. This effect can be further accentuated by adding a little gesso, which can be worked into and when dry makes an excellent surface for watercolor painting.

Knifing out

The principle of knifing out is that the blade has a squeegee effect, compressing the surface and pushing the paint to one side where it collects. For flexible lines, use a pointed painting knife. If you hold it on its side, you will also be able to remove large areas of paint. A palette knife, with its rounded point, creates wider lines. For even bigger areas, a credit card works well; an old one can be cut to suitable sizes.

Timing is crucial. If you knife a fine line when the paint is very wet, you will get a dark line as the paper will be bruised and the paint will flood into the groove (although a large area will displace all right). To get a white line out of the paint it must be damp; the paint will then evacuate the groove, leaving an almost clean line.

1 With a pencil sketch complete, do an underpainting using ultramarine in the sky, yellow ocher for the building, and violet for the dome. Follow this with a mix of viridian and yellow ocher for the surrounding vegetation.

2 Use a plastic spatula to apply gesso to the areas that you want to scour into (stonework, vegetation, etc.). While this is wet use the end of the brush handle to make linear impressions in the gesso and let this dry.

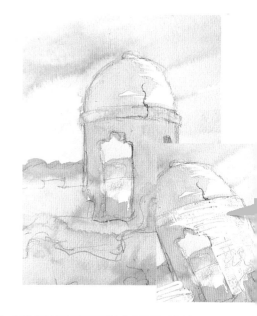

VARIATION • I
Painting knife

1 *Using Prussian blue, yellow ocher, and a little burnt sienna, paint the background, face, hair, and shirt. Let this sink into the paper and, while it is still slightly damp, lightly scrape out highlights with the tip of a painting knife.*

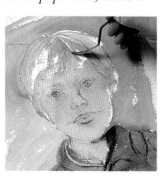

2 *While the underpainting is still damp, use a No. 9 brush to paint in some shadows on the face with burnt sienna and into the hair with burnt umber. Slight softening of the edges will occur.*

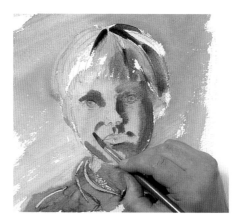

3 *The darker paint on the hair makes an excellent surface out of which to knife strands of hair. If you knife out while the paint is too wet, it will flood back into the groove, leaving a darker line. This effect may be used to advantage in some cases.*

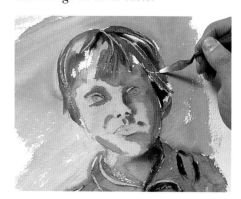

3 Paint over the stonework with yellow ocher, viridian, and brown madder alizarin. The lines appear dark as the paint settles in the grooves.

4 Using the same colors, continue to build up the scene, painting directly over the gesso areas, as you would paper. Add a second wash of ultramarine to the sky and use it to paint all the shaded areas to the right of the turret and below.

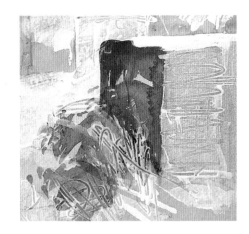

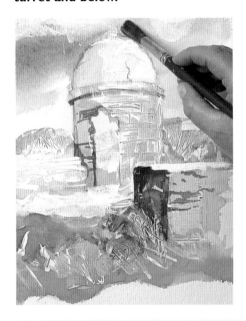

5 Paint all the detail on the walls and the shaded part of the dome in violet with a No. 3 round brush. Give the distant shrubs more definition with viridian and a little yellow ocher.

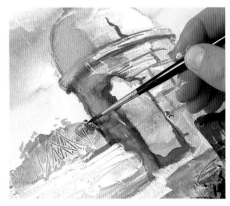

6 The use of a limited palette with only a minimum of color mixing gives this painting a fresh feeling. The knifed out gesso gives an important added dimension of texture, which combined with the clear colors makes an energetic and enchanting result.

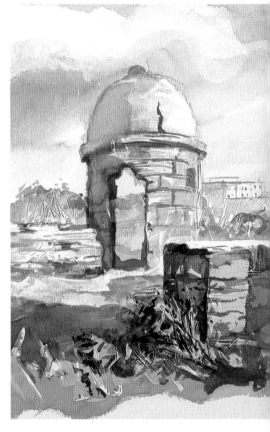

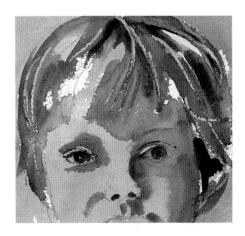

4 *This close up shows the soft serrated edges of the knifed-out lines, in keeping with the overall effect. The knife's flexible blade can also be used to achieve curved tapering lines.*

5 *Knifing out can give a simple painting some key directional lines, which suggest detail and add movement without being obtrusive. It is an excellent way of avoiding painstaking brushwork, which carries the danger of overworking.*

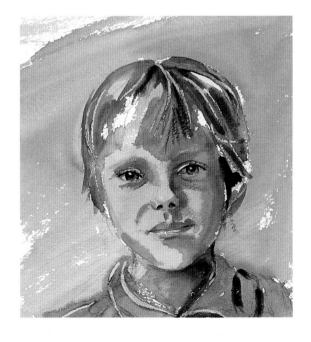

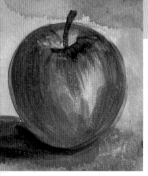

As already described in *Building Up* (see page 52), glazing is fundamental to watercolor work, and is produced by the transparency of the medium. This quality can be taken further with the aid of glazing media which will increase transparency, adding a rich luster and a glassy sheen. The quality of watercolor glazing is particularly favorable for achieving skin tones.

Gum arabic layers

As the name implies, glazing is similar to layers of colored glass. The white paper reflects the light through each glaze of color. Gum arabic allows paint to retain transparency over a greater number of layers. Be sure to dry the paint between each glaze and don't overwork each layer. Try and lay each color in one positive brushstroke.

Glazing

Gum arabic is an excellent glazing medium, imparting a glossy varnish to the surface which greatly enriches the color. It is less likely to disturb paint underneath than paint diluted with water that will dissolve under-layers causing softening of the edges and reducing the crispness of the image. Aquapasto is a much thicker glaze medium, suitable for dry-brush glazing. A glaze medium increases the transparency of opaque colors such as Chinese white and Naples yellow, while allowing them to retain their thick consistency and so providing more control. There's no limit to the number of glazes you can apply because each one deepens the color and progressively darkens the image. You should choose colors carefully to avoid muddying and loss of freshness in your work.

1 **It's not essential to use gum Arabic in the first wash – the full fluidity of water is enough to create a softly blended underpainting. Use raw sienna, burnt sienna, and Winsor green in the hair, cadmium red with Naples yellow for the skin. Leave to dry.**

2 **Now mix together gum arabic, a little water, and burnt sienna. Paint over the hair again with brushstrokes that follow the direction of the hair. The thickness of the gum arabic will cause some brushstrokes to break up. This is specially effective over the top of the head, suggesting reflected light. Leave to dry.**

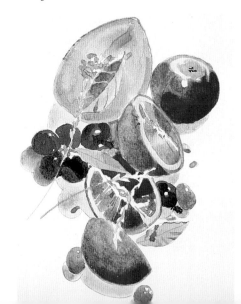

VARIATION • 1
Concentrated gum arabic

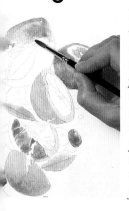

1 *When gum arabic is used in very concentrated form throughout, it imparts a pleasing blotchy texture as it comes into contact with the paper surface. Use Hooker's green, yellow gamboge, and alizarin crimson with undiluted gum arabic for the first washes.*

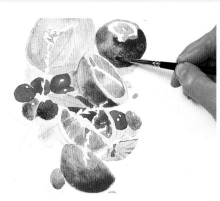

2 *Paint the grapes with Winsor blue. Then glaze a second coat over each color in selected areas, largely covering the oranges, but only with touches on the melon, leaves, and grapes.*

3 *Finish off with a third glaze over the darker parts of the oranges. Complete all of the details.*

3 Use Prussian blue and spectrum yellow without gum arabic to lay a wash over the background. Add further glazes of Winsor green and raw sienna, mixed with gum arabic and a little burnt sienna over the hair. Paint cadmium red mixed with gum arabic on the face. Add detail to sharpen the features.

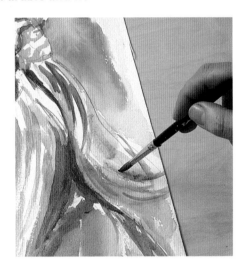

5 The finished portrait shows how gum arabic has imparted a rich luster and great depth of tone to the hair.

4 Paint almost pure gum arabic with a touch of alizarin crimson in streaks over parts of the hair, followed by a little Prussian blue. The final glazes can be with pure gum arabic and no water. Paint the hair ribbon and sweater in a loose wash of cadmium red with no gum arabic.

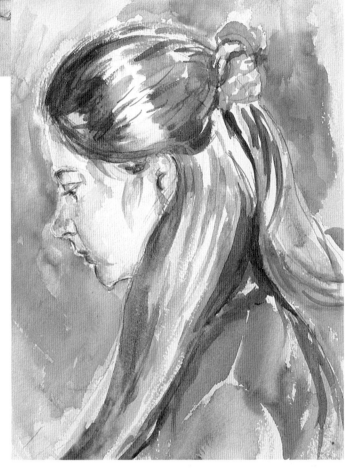

VARIATION • 2
Aquapasto

1 *Paint the initial washes, diluted just with water for maximum coverage. Leave to dry. Then mix aquapasto with equal parts of water and burnt sienna to a creamy consistency, and glaze the mix over the horse.*

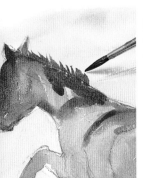

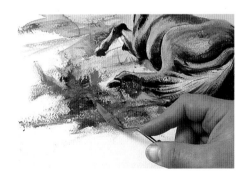

2 *Gradually build up the glazes using ever-thicker paint containing more aquapasto and less water. Finally mix some pigment with aquapasto only. This is very buttery and will be easier to apply with a palette knife.*

3 *This finished painting employs the complete spectrum of consistencies, from pure water to pure aquapasto. However, a certain amount of transparency is retained throughout.*

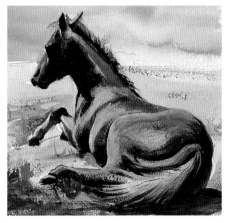

In context

Knifing out, glazing, the use of body color, and scraping back are seen in the broad context of finished paintings. The four different artists whose work is featured can be seen to have different preferences and work in different ways. An artist may use only a few techniques in any one painting, but in the course of their career will probably make use of most techniques.

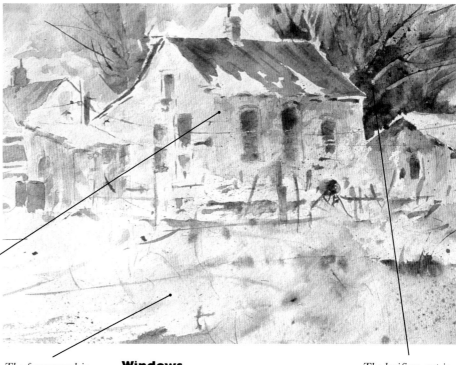

The house is painted with one wash for the walls and one wash for the roof. The windows and door are hinted at with single brushstrokes. Each brushmark is carefully executed to fulfill its task.

The foreground is largely left as white paper. Only very pale, loose washes have been applied, with a little spatter and freehand pencil lines. The eye is directed straight to the house.

Windows

James Harvey Taylor

This painting is a good example of how a specific technique can be ideally suited to a particular style of painting. This picture is executed with a charming economy of brushwork that is treated with fluency and dynamism. Knifing out is the perfect method for rendering detail without fussiness.

The knifing out is confined to this corner where it is used to describe the pale branches of the winter trees. The sweeping curves extend out of the picture.

Tuolumne Pool

Dan Peterson

This painting shows clearly how you can glaze over a whole area of detail without disturbing the underlying pigment and yet completely change the effect. The glazing demonstrates the transparency of watercolor, fully exploited to create richness and a truly convincing illusion of depth.

The deep blues of the rocks are achieved by superimposing several layers of paint.

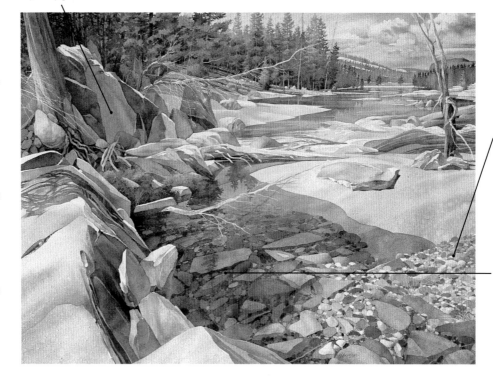

All the pebbles were this color before the final glaze was applied over those in the center. The unglazed pebbles are much paler and the whites are still evident.

To create this rock pool the pebbles were painted first. When they were dry, a warm mix of paint was quickly washed over, leaving out the tips of a few boulders, which protruded above the surface.

Flowers on a Table
Maurice Read

In this painting body color, or gouache, is used in conjunction with watercolor. Each type of paint plays a complementary role. The soft flowing translucence of watercolor is suitable for the background and foreground, while the dense, bright colors of gouache are ideal for the flowers.

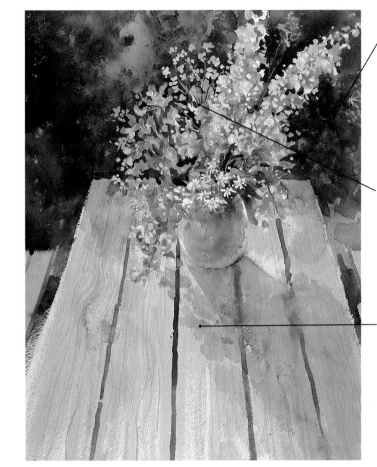

The background is a build-up of fairly concentrated dark green and black watercolor washes. Minute chinks of light can be seen breaking through.

Some white paper was reserved for the flowers. Watercolor was used for the initial washes. Thick gouache was overpainted for most of the brightest petals.

The foreground table area is treated with several super-imposed pale wash-es but remains clear, fresh, and uncluttered.

Les Bateaux
E Gordon West

The scraping back in this exciting painting is done with great skill. The way the sharp blade has scraped the painted surface, leaving minute dots and tears, creates a stunning shimering effect. The ripples stand out so clearly against the inky black water that even the tiniest lines are visible.

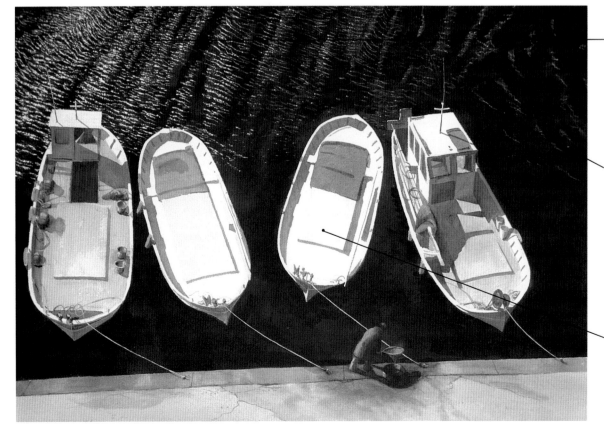

The sheer volume of scraped-back lines causes this area to radiate with light. The lines are careful to follow the calm ripples of water. As the ripples get brighter, more pressure is needed on the scalpel blade.

The ripples are still evident, with hair-line marks scraped back with such gentle pressure that only the dots appear as the blade catches the crests of the paper texture.

The boats are virtually all white paper. The minimal detail is nevertheless applied with great accuracy. The aerial view and the strong contrasts are the strength of this composition.

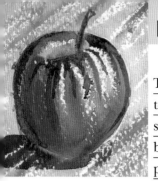

This is an unusual technique yielding surprising results, based on the principle that wax repels water. Exciting rippled textures can be created with linear control, from fine lines to broad areas. Wax resist can convey a wide range of subjects, including sea foam, bark, rock surfaces, and even complete branches.

Wax resist

Household candles are highly suitable for wax-resist work as they are transparent and can be laid over white paper or another color. The marks they make remain invisible until the next wash that will be displaced as the wax magically reveals its presence. You can sharpen the candle to a fine point, or cut it into other shapes. For an overall texture, use the side of the candle. The result you achieve depends largely on the paper's surface texture. Rough paper, for example, will produce a coarse, grainy effect as the wax adheres to the high spots and the paint settles in the hollows. Wax color crayons work in the same way and impart lovely granular lines. Oil pastels are exactly the same except that the colors are stronger.

Transparent wax

Make a candle into an effective drawing tool by sharpening one end with a sharp knife. This will give much more control to the application of wax to the paper. In this picture wax resist is used to portray the foam and spray of the falling water. Use a cold-pressed or rough surfaced paper to help convey the rough textures that are suited to this subject.

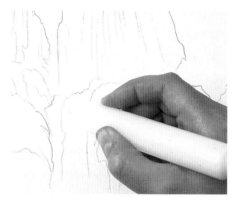

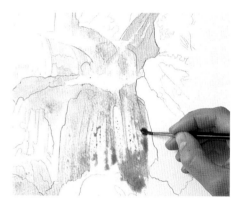

1 Rub vertical strokes of the candle in the direction of the water. Be careful not to apply too much wax as it is difficult to remove. If you do need to remove wax, however, this can be done using an iron and brown paper.

2 Paint over the water area with a mix of cobalt blue deep and magenta. The waxed areas, which resist the paint, appear as white strips. Paint the surrounding bank with pale washes of Hooker's green and gamboge.

VARIATION • 1
Wax crayons

1 *Make a pencil drawing of the subject. Use red and green wax crayons to draw in the detail of the flower petals, leaves, and stalks. Paint over the petals with a pale wash of cadmium red deep, and over the leaves and stalks with cobalt green.*

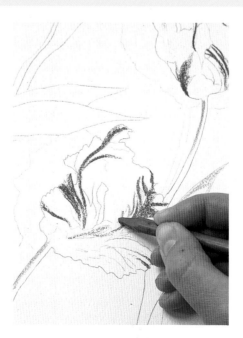

2 *The wax crayon resisted the paint, leaving textured lines over pale washes. Use blue crayon and watercolor wash in the same way, but apply the blue in softer hatching rather than strong lines.*

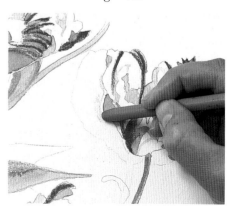

3 Add some Hooker's green to the water area and to the large central mossy stone. Let the edges blend together softly. Paint black, cerulean blue, and Hooker's green on the right bank.

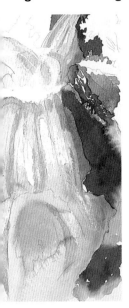

4 Continue to build up the mossy bank with further applications of gamboge and Hooker's green. Add cobalt blue to the water in several glazes. Encourage a mixture of soft blending and sharper variable edges for cleaner definition.

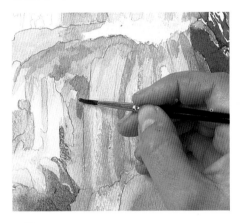

5 The final painting reveals a comprehensive build-up of translucent glazes. The wax has resisted the paint throughout, retaining the clean white of the underlying paper, highlighted by the application of deeper color.

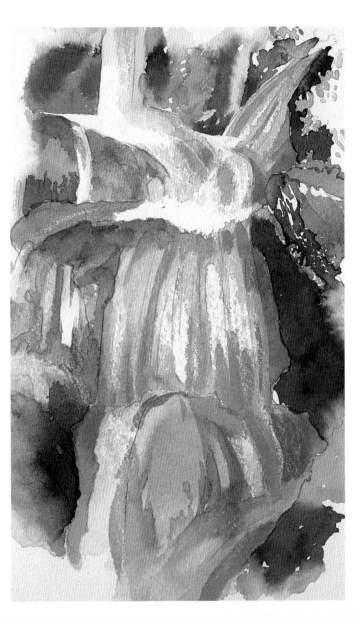

3 Create pleasing irregular shapes by applying a wash of cobalt blue mixed with a little cadmium red deep over some of the blue wax areas.

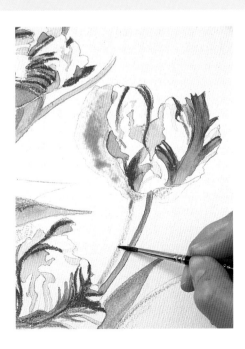

4 Complete the flowers with a gamboge wash. In this painting the pale washes enhance the rich textured lines of the wax crayon underdrawing to produce a highly decorative effect.

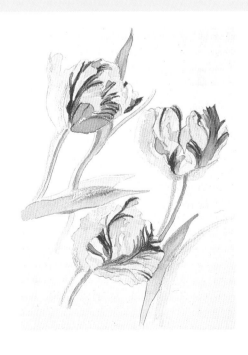

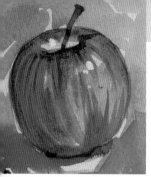

A toned ground is a painting surface that is already evenly colored in a pale shade. This can have distinct advantages. Due to the transparency of watercolor, the paper color will influence practically all subsequent layers of paint. This creates a distinct color bias, unifying the whole painting and helping to create wonderfully atmospheric pictures.

Toned ground

Tinted papers are available in warm or cool shades. They can also be made by laying an overall flat acrylic wash (see Small Flat Wash, page 32). The color tints you choose will determine the eventual outcome of the painting, so color and subject matter must be compatible. (This is not so evident with opaque paint.) Because the basic color scheme is already established, the overall painting becomes simpler. If left unpainted, the paper color also plays a role. To achieve lighter colors than the paper, a body color (see page 122) must be used, and this can be extremely effective. The only drawback to using a tinted ground is that some colors will not show – for example, lemon yellow won't show up on blue paper. Unless it's opaque yellow, it will optically mix to produce a green tinge (see Glazing, page 128).

Warm acrylic ground

Acrylic paint can be diluted and used as a wash much like watercolor with one important difference: when it is dry it will not dissolve with subsequent painting, which makes it an ideal ground. It also leaves a smooth working surface that will easily accept watercolor.

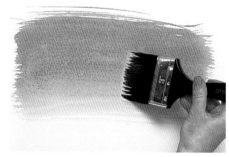

1 Mix sufficient cadmium yellow acrylic with Napthol red light acrylic to complete the wash. Using a large decorator's brush, paint over the whole paper surface, extending beyond its edges. Spread the paint evenly, working backward and forward.

2 It may be necessary to stroke over the wash with a piece of kitchen paper, to even out the varying concentrations of color. When you have achieved an even color of the right intensity, let it dry thoroughly. If a darker color is needed, repeat the process.

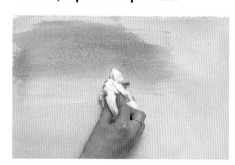

VARIATION • 1
Cool tinted ground

1 Stain the paper surface with a pale wash of viridian and cobalt blue. After you have completed the pencil drawing, use gamboge followed by Prussian blue and alizarin crimson to paint the shells. Apply simple flat washes with a little wet-in-wet mingling.

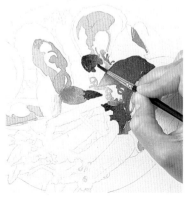

2 Paint the shadow of the plate with cobalt green in an even flat wash using a No. 3 round sable. This color harmonizes with the pale green background.

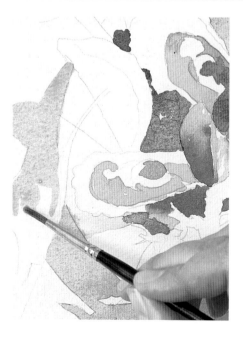

3 Paint over the acrylic wash in the normal way. Use cerulean blue for the distant mountains and alizarin crimson and Prussian blue for the nearer ones. Wash over the sky with cadmium yellow and cadmium red.

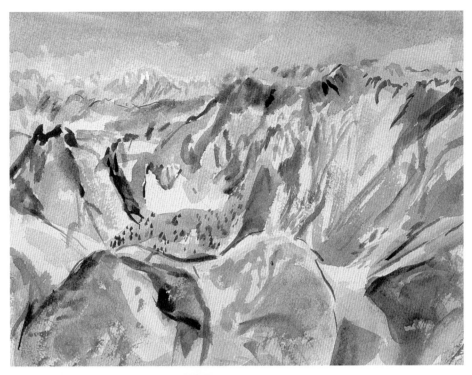

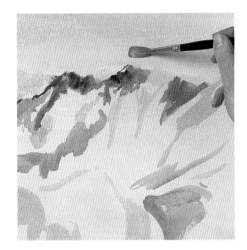

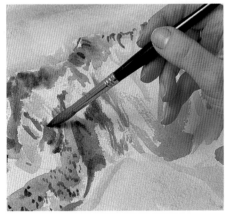

4 Using the same colors, continue to build up the mountains with fluid brushstrokes. Leave some of the ground unpainted, as this creates a warm tone that permeates the whole scene.

5 Apply small dabs of Chinese white to indicate the distant snow-capped mountains and as pale streaks in the sky for clouds. Although only a little white is used, its effect is enormous. Its opacity stands out in cool contrast, completing this evocative painting.

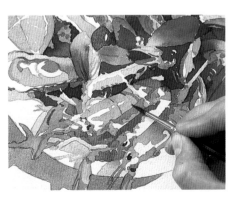

3 Gradually build up the color areas, methodically laying down flat washes. Overlay the green shadow with Hooker's green. Add cobalt blue deep to the mussels and paint the lobsters with magenta, gamboge, and alizarin crimson.

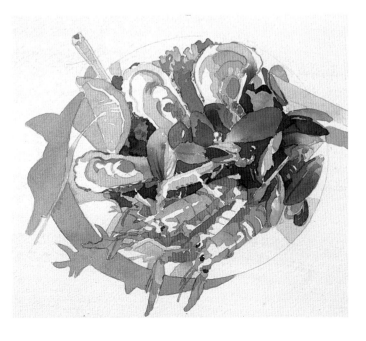

4 The cool green of the ground causes the bright yellows and reds to stand out in contrast and "vibrate." These opposing color values create a dynamic tension. The tinted background also imparts a depth that could not be achieved with stark white paper.

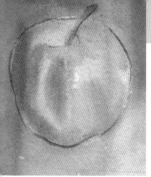

Washing off

If a painting goes badly wrong, rather than scrap the paper you can wash the whole picture. As the pigments dissolve and dissipate, interesting effects appear and a ghost image is left that you can work over. This gives you a second chance to paint the subject.

Wash out dried paint preferably under warm running water or submerge the paper fully. A decorator's brush will help dislodge the paint, but be gentle to minimize damage to the surface which is more vulnerable when wet. A heavy paper will cope better with this treatment, but if you have used a light-weight paper (140 lb or less) you should rinse it while still on the board then re-stretch it. Some colors will come off more easily than others. Staining colors such as pthalo blue will hang on tenaciously, in which case you can use a little bleach, leaving it on for a short time then rinsing it off. Sedimentary colors such as manganese blue will disappear almost completely.

Fully submerged

Without any experimentation, you won't learn new techniques, but if a painting is not turning out how you hoped, there is no point in continuing. You can start again on a fresh piece of paper, you can turn the paper over, or you can wash off your picture.

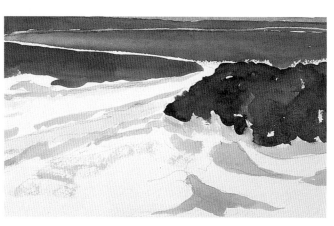

1 **This painting is a perfect candidate for washing off, allowing you to change your mind and convert this sea view into a desert scene.**

2 **Trim the paper to fit into a sink, bath or bowl. Slide it under the water and leave it to soak for a few minutes. Cartridge paper responds almost instantaneously. Heavyweight paper will need a little longer.**

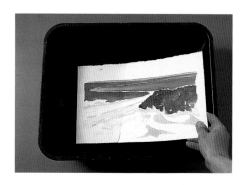

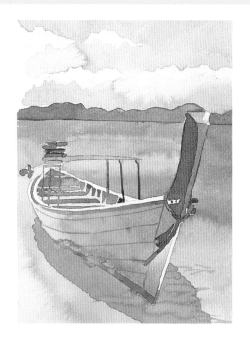

VARIATION • 1
Under hot running water

1 *This is a pretty painting, but there are many reasons you may have to wash it off. For example, you may want to simply soften the image slightly, leaving a dream-like, ghost image – indeed some artists make a feature of this.*

2 *Hold the picture under hot running water. The heat will help to remove some of the more tenacious stain colors such as phthalo blue. Move the picture from side to side, allowing the water to cover the whole area.*

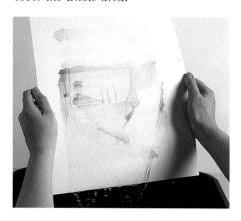

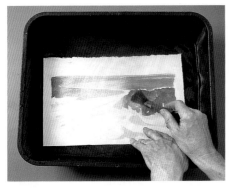

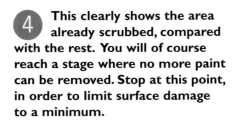

4 This clearly shows the area already scrubbed, compared with the rest. You will of course reach a stage where no more paint can be removed. Stop at this point, in order to limit surface damage to a minimum.

3 After a while the pigments will begin to dissolve. Take a decorater's brush with long flexible hair that isn't too abrasive. Work over the surface in a circular motion. Heavyweight paper can take a lot of scrubbing, but be very gentle with thin paper.

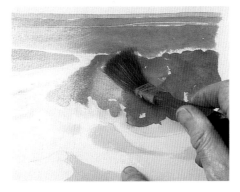

5 The previous image is barely visible and will have little impact on a new painting. You could, of course, include it to enhance an underpainting.

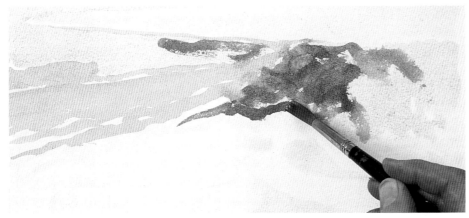

6 Re-stretch the paper. It's advisable to re-stretch even the heavyweight paper, as it will probably have buckled slightly. Unless you want to work straight into a wet surface, wait for the paper to dry. You can now begin your new picture, even using a completely different color scheme as shown here.

3 *After a few minutes, you will notice a huge difference. You can stop when the result suits your needs. Most of the paint will come off in the first few minutes, but with patience almost all will disappear.*

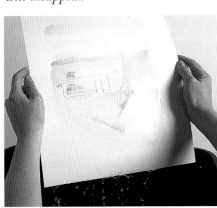

4 *As before, you will need to re-stretch the paper and leave it to dry. Notice how some colors are still slightly visible and others have completely disappeared. This demonstrates how colors all have slightly different staining properties.*

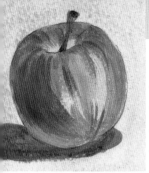

Several additives can be included in the mixing process that change a paint's consistency, increasing or decreasing its fluidity. If you thicken the mixture, it becomes more controllable and easier to glaze; it also makes dry-brush easier (see page 86). By increasing fluidity, you will allow it to blend in unpredictable ways, creating exciting effects.

Liquid aids

If you mix almost pure gum arabic with pigment, the paint becomes viscous. When painted onto a dry surface, it's not quickly absorbed by the paper, and so there is more time for manipulation and blending. On a wet surface the flow of paint will be sluggish, creating soft furry edges. Ox gall liquid accelerates fluidity. In particular, if the pigment is mixed only with ox gall, and the paper surface is dampened with ox gall, a magical effect is produced as tendrils spread out in all directions. Dishwashing (washing-up) liquid creates similar effects to gum arabic but without the glossy appearance. It leaves a slightly blotchy finish that can be useful.

Dishwashing liquid

Dishwashing liquid is a mat version of gum arabic. It slows down excessive fluidity in wet-in-wet painting. If overworked, it will froth up but this frothing will subside as it dries. Its overall effect is to create a soft-focus painting. Always use a clear, colorless dishwashing liquid.

1 Mix permanent green deep with almost completely undiluted liquid. Using a medium round brush, paint the left-hand bush and overhanging creeper. As the paint dries, the pigment will settle into a granulated texture.

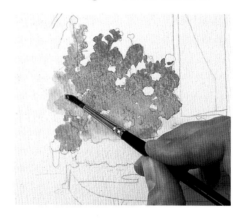

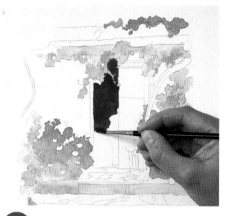

2 Before the creeper has completely dried, paint the open door with Winsor blue and dishwashing liquid. The two will very slowly blend a little due to the thick consistency of the soap, resulting in a soft, furry edge.

VARIATION • 1
Gum arabic

1 *Gum arabic works in a similar way to dishwashing liquid, except that it dries with a glossy sheen, like a varnish, which greatly enriches the colors. Mix gum arabic with cobalt blue deep and paint the jugs and vase, omitting white areas for the flowery patterns and other colors.*

2 *Paint the patterns and flowers with combinations of yellow gamboge, black, magenta, and cerulean blue. Again use gum arabic as the medium with little or no water.*

3 *The finished composition is simple with emphasis on patterns, limited molding, and mainly flat colors. The most exciting aspect is the texture produced by the glutinous gum arabic as it separates the blue pigment.*

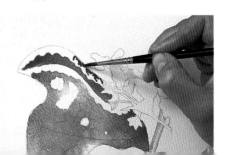

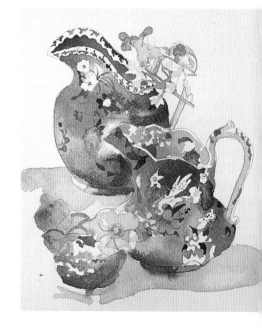

3 Paint the shadows of the overhead vines in Winsor blue mixed with alizarin crimson and dishwashing liquid. Paint the dark shadow on the door with a mix of Winsor blue and black.

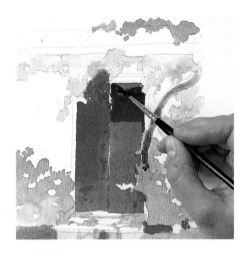

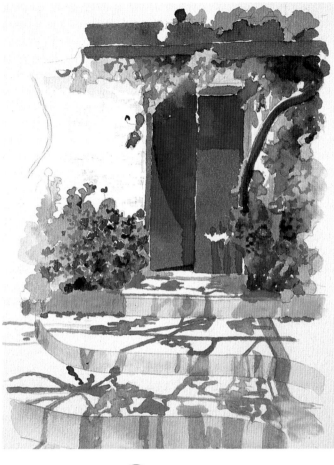

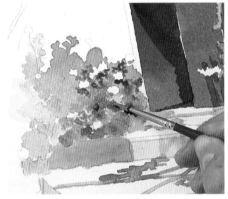

4 Overpaint the greenery with a darker mix of color and dishwashing liquid. This is the final application to the plants, so suggest a few leaves and vary the intensity of the color.

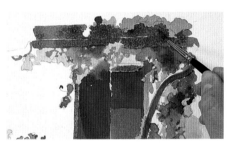

5 Mix alizarin crimson, Winsor blue, and black, and paint the overhead pergola, allowing it to fuse a little with the vine. Notice the blotchy texture produced by the soap; this effect diminishes a little on drying.

6 Using dishwashing liquid to control the paint is well suited to this careful style of painting. It also increases the paint's transparency, making it suitable for glazing, as well as softening the edges.

VARIATION • 2
Ox gall liquid

1 *Paint the background with Prussian blue, in a loose, broken wash. Mix ox gall liquid with Prussian blue and add this wet-in-wet to the wash in several places. Accelerated bleeding and fusion of paint will occur in those places.*

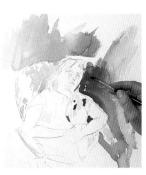

2 *Add more Prussian blue and a mix of Winsor green and raw sienna, both with ox gall liquid, to the background. Build up the skin tones with raw sienna, burnt sienna, and a little cadmium red. Paint cerulean blue on the chairs and clothes.*

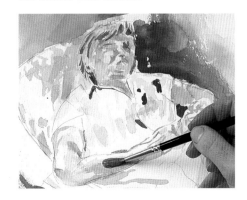

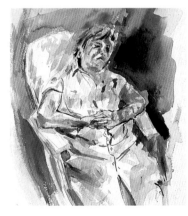

3 *The action of the ox gall liquid is more evident on the background, with some dramatic effects. There is an interesting paradox between the man resting and the dynamic tension expressed in the brushwork.*

In context

These three paintings have the seashore in common, but are produced in slightly different ways. An important variation is that two are painted on a toned ground and one is on normal white paper. The two that are painted on toned grounds use body color to a great degree. Observe how the painting on white paper has a much brighter feel, without the need for opaque highlights.

Shoreham Mudflats
Mark Topham

Apart from the significant amount of white body color used, this is an entirely watercolor painting, executed on a tinted handmade watercolor paper. The beige ground could be mistaken for wash, except that it permeates the whole painting and in no place is white paper seen.

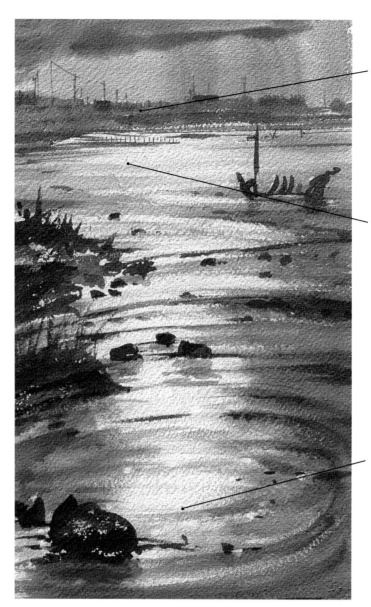

The blue washes are muted slightly by the color of the ground. Colors similar to that of the ground need to be darkened slightly.

In some places the ground is left exposed. Small patches of bare ground can be seen all over the painting.

Thick white body color was applied using a dry-brush technique to represent the reflected moonlight. It appears startlingly bright. Care must be taken not to overdo this effect.

The wax was rubbed on thinly here. Individual streaks are visible.

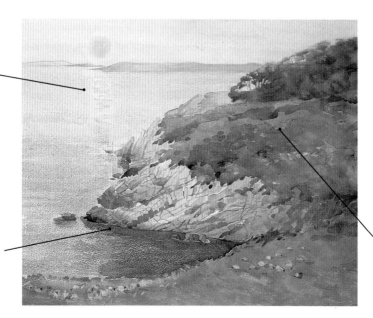

A high concentration of wax was applied in this area. The wash is concentrated to further accentuate the grainy texture.

Evening, Silverdale, Lancashire
Maurice Read

Wax resist is the key technique in this painting. It is used in an unobtrusive and distinctive way to render the grainy texture of the sea. Usually wax is rubbed on like a crayon and can be seen in lines. Here it has been rubbed on in broad sideways strokes to cover a wide area. The watercolor wash was applied over the top.

The landscape was painted in the normal way, with wet washes, creating a smooth paint surface.

The gray ground dominates the sky and where the paint is similar in tone, the effect is that of a pastel painting.

A concentrated white has been used to obliterate the gray ground. The color of the paint remains pure because there is no underpainting that could sully the overlaid paint.

Brodick Bay, Arran

Maurice Read

This painting is done on fairly dark gray card, which has a smooth surface. The paints used included a high proportion of opaque gouache colors. Although the style is that of watercolor painting, the gouache paints are more prominent. As usual with toned ground paintings, the ground color is allowed to feature strongly, having a marked influence on all the colors.

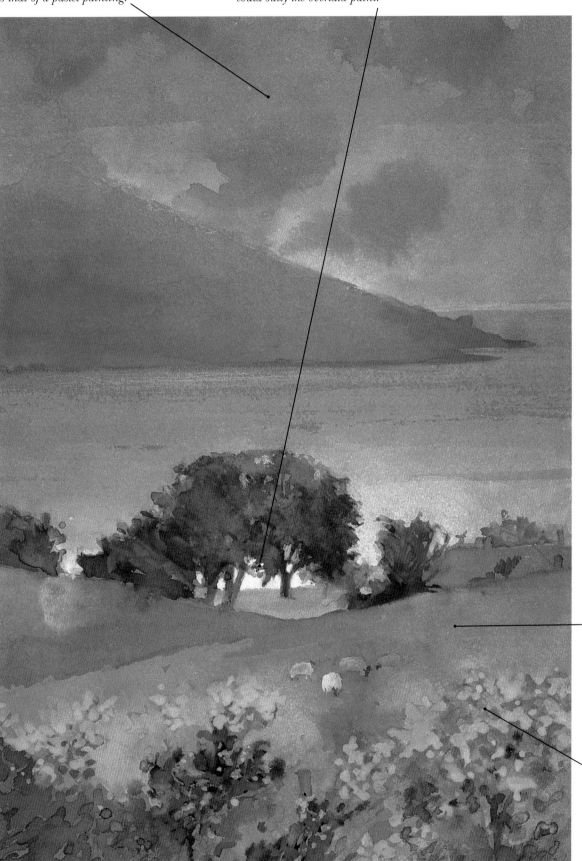

These gouache greens appear fresh and bright, but they are in fact greatly muted by the neutralizing effect of the gray ground. A watercolor green would have been much weaker.

The yellows and violets of the foreground flowers are painted thickly in gouache over underpainted green. In contrast to the subdued colors all around, they appear bright and radiant.

INDEX

CREDITS

Quarto would like to thank the
following artists who took part in
the demonstrations:

Rima Bray
Jean Cantor
Patrick Cullen
Nicola Gregory
Valerie Hill
Terry Longhurst
Debra Manifold
Steve Nicol
Alan Oliver
Mark Topham
Sue Ellen Wilder

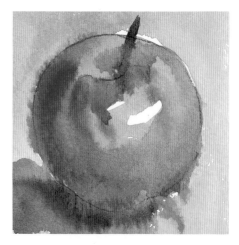

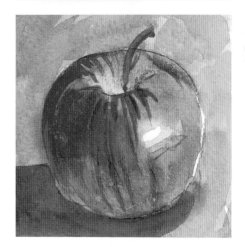

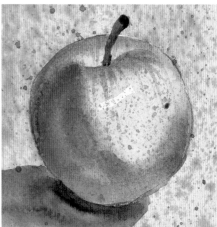

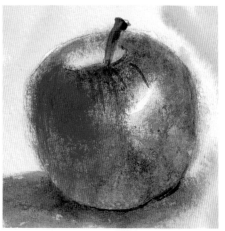